TODAY'S INSPIRED

Leader

Volume IV

TODAY'S INSPIRED LEADER VOLUME IV

This book is a compilation of stories from people who have contributed a chapter and is designed to provide inspiration to our readers.

It is sold with the understanding that the publisher and the individual authors are not engaged in the rendering of psychological, legal, accounting or other professional advice. The content and views in each chapter are the sole expression and opinion of its author and not necessarily the views of Fig Factor Media, LLC.

For more information, contact:

Fig Factor Media, LLC | www.figfactormedia.com
Today's Inspired Leader | www.todaysleader.com

Cover Design by Juan Pablo Ruiz
Layout by LDG Juan Manuel Serna Rosales

Printed in the United States of America

FIG FACTOR MEDIA

ISBN: 978-1-957058-93-1
Library of Congress Control Number: 2022922275

To all that answer the call of leadership

CONTENTS

ACKNOWLEDGMENTS

Special thanks to all the leaders that have believed in me when I did not even believe in myself. To my parents whose relentless support has created a sense of service in my heart. To my kids Giullianna and Leo who teach me to live fully every day.

PREFACE
By Diana Martinez

The greatest gift any leader can offer is to inspire, empower, and encourage the team to contribute to give people the opportunity to contribute to the organization in a meaningful way. People are motivated to work on something greater than themselves that will make a difference, and it is the leader's role to provide the support and opportunity and then empower them to "take the ball and run!"

When you look back on the jobs you've loved, you most likely made a significant contribution or feel like you've made a difference, we remember those positive experiences. Meaningful work propels us to do other projects and possibly take on a leadership role. That's one reason people spend a lot of time volunteering, for example. They donate hours and hours of their time and talent because they want to make a difference and believe in an organization's mission.

As a leader in the workplace, when you give your people a chance to contribute in a meaningful way and support them and give them the tools they need, you give birth to new leaders.

I would describe leadership as a gift that should be taken seriously. A leader influences so many people, and that impact can make or break their day, week or career. If you can help them to reach their potential, they become great opportunities for both the organization and the individuals involved.

Leadership is not about you; it's about the people you're

leading. Personally, I've always led in a very collaborative way since I work in the performing arts arena. Some of my positions include being the executive director of the Paramount Theater in Aurora, Illinois; the director of entertainment and marketing at the former Pheasant Run Resort in St. Charles, Illinois; and my current role as director of College of DuPage's McAninch Arts Center in Glen Ellyn, Illinois.

From 2009 to 2012, I was fortunate to work as president of The Second City in Chicago, well-known around the country as being the home of improvisational comedy in the Midwest. The people there had a famous expression "Yes, and…" This is about never saying no. To be clear, it's not just saying yes to everything you hear, but it's about being open to new ideas and acknowledging and affirming them so they feel like they are listened to and validated.

Many people think that those in our industry are just innately creative. It doesn't really work that way; you have to create the time and space to be creative. When leaders want innovation and creativity, they have to look in the mirror and say, "Well, what am I doing to foster creativity?" "Am I having meetings to foster innovation? Am I listening? Am I providing the opportunity not only to succeed, but also to fail because not everything works out the very first time?" You have to create safe environments to fail. That's where you test pilot concepts to learn of their potential viability.

Leaders genuinely have an impact on others. Reflecting on my own experiences, I had the opportunity to meet actors and directors who were nascent in their careers and have become famous for their craft in their own right. I worked with Katrina Lenk, who won a Tony award in 2018 for "The Band's Visit" and had a role in the television series "Ozark." I directed Anna Chlumsky who people know from the "My Girl" movies and from "Veep." Locally, I know Melissa Mercado, executive director of Fox Valley Music Foundation dba The Venue and Lara Filip, executive director of Inkwell Arts and Learning Co, who presents Walking Plays for Morton Arboretum in Lisle, Illinois. Sean Hayes of "Will & Grace" was my musical director at Pheasant Run for many years. Chris Witaske was an intern for me, and he created a Netflix series called "Chicago Party Aunt."

Leaders show by example from the moment they walk into the office. If you walk by somebody, don't say hello or you're not in tune with them, they might be offended. As a leader, you aren't entitled to have a bad day. You always have to put on your game face and forge ahead. For example, I was heavily involved in presenting a Frida Kahlo exhibit at the College of DuPage, and then the COVID-19 pandemic hit. We had to stop our musical and theatrical performances. I was terrified because many theater troupes were laying off people, and I wondered if this would happen to our staff. Instead of worrying and wondering, I took action. I said to my staff that we're going to do online productions. We researched doing a socially distanced performance done by a 60-piece symphony orchestra outside in the winter, with heaters and using instrument masks to block the spread of airborne particles. These solutions worked, and we were able to keep the season going.

Being a leader means that you also have to be innovative when there are challenges and put your people first. You always have to fulfill your mission first and keep the best interests of the people working for you. They have to feel from their leader that they are valued and respected; otherwise, they're not going to be invested in your mission.

The most important thing you can give to someone is the opportunity to contribute in a meaningful way. I looked back at a time when someone took a chance on me when I graduated from college and also when I took a risk. In 1988, the person running Pheasant Run's Theater Department died, and the resort was searching for a replacement. The general manager came to see a show I produced and asked me to talk with him the following week. I presented an idea of how the resort should be doing a musical theater dinner season like those done at Marriott, Drury Lane, and Candlelight Theater. He liked my work and my idea and hired me. When he learned that I was only 22, he rescinded his offer.

I was devastated because these were my ideas and concepts, and my age was no reflection on the hard work I spent in the theater. I made a deal with him. I said I will do the first show for free, and if that made money, we'd split the profits. The show sold out, and it extended its run. I became the director of the resort's entertainment and marketing for 13 years.

The last thing that leaders can do is to ask themselves these questions: "How do you leave something better than you found it? How do you positively impact as many people as possible?"

It's not just about being successful, but what are the residual effects of success. If these effects hurt somebody, then it's not such a great plan. You really have to look at the whole picture and now only how it's affecting you or the bottom line but the general community and your fellow collaborators. The more people you bring to the table, the better the ideas. The bigger the table gets, the more there is to manage, but I also think the better and richer the situation becomes. When you have all those people contributing, they are working to something much more greater than they can could ever do on their own.

Diana Martinez
Director of McAninch Arts Center at College of DuPage

INTRODUCTION
By Jacqueline S. Ruiz

Some say that leaders are born, some say leaders are made. In the year of 2018, I had an opportunity to take a 250-hour course on leadership that forever changed my perspective. The most complete body of work that I had experienced in my life; created by Henry Givray. Every session was separated by six weeks to allow the participants time to read books, internalize the content and live the principles. From March to October, my entire mind was set around the concept of leadership.

It was there where I learned that leaders are neither born or made. Leaders are called upon. Anyone can rise up to leadership on any given moment. A child responding a certain way to a situation could be a leader, a teacher making a decision to instill principles in his/her students can be a leader, a bystander stopping by to help someone can be a leader. I learned that leadership is all about our actions and reactions. It is about how gracefully we handle a situation and how we elevate others in the process. I learned that leadership is about a realization of responsibility in a given situation. It is about honoring the best outcome for all involved. It is about emotional intelligence.

Along the side of this life-changing course, I had the opportunity to secure my pilot's license. Coincidentally both paths aligned with the same principles of self-evaluation and self-managing. As I got to know myself more, I became a better leader and pilot. The more that I found out about my fears and triggers, the more that I was able to make better decisions on the ground and in the air. At the end, it was about knowledge and self-awareness. You see, when you are piloting an airplane as the pilot in command, the awesome responsibility of landing falls on you, the same way that answering the call to leadership falls on you, especially if life is presenting with you an opportunity to respond.

As you read these pages, my hope is that every one of these extraordinary individuals that answers the call to leadership and continue to do so, may inspire you to take your next move. Scientists, mathematicians, business executives, entrepreneurs, financial experts will share their insights about leadership and how they are showing up with their congruent actions.

May you answer the call to leadership in your every day.

LEADERSHIP IS IN MY DNA

Adriana Rozo-Angulo

"Every day, I take time to thank God for everything I have. I do this while I'm in the shower and there are no distractions."

I have been a natural leader since childhood, and it has always felt like leadership is in my DNA. No matter what task or challenge is before me, I am driven to navigate my way through it. I look at the problem before me, and I can see the path that needs to be followed.

Not only am I a problem solver who leads others and helps accomplish goals, but I am also a Christian. My strong faith gives my life purpose and ensures that my leadership is born of knowledge and desire to help, not power.

This leadership style has developed in me from when I was young and in the Scouts, chosen as the leader because I knew instinctively how to organize a team. I organized everything—my room, my family, anywhere I went. I have always solved problems for myself and others. I would think about the challenge and say, "Ok, this is what we need to do." Then, I would outline the steps and get everyone assigned to do their part. With time, I learned to like managing situations. As I got older, I grew as a leader and in my faith as a Christian. While I honed my leadership skills through experience and training, at church I learned that God gave me this gift and was calling me to be a servant leader.

In servant leadership, I discovered that I needed to be a servant first and a leader second, which is how I look at life today. How can I help others using what I know and what I have? For me, it's a conscious choice. If I want to lead, I have to be the servant first. It has become the way I live, at home and work. It's thoughtful, deliberate, and action based.

Don't mistake me for shy or quiet, though. I'm a small woman who is 5'1" with a strong personality and a Hispanic heritage, and I have a big accent when speaking English. I've always felt the need to prove that I'm capable of whatever I want to do, especially in the corporate environment. This was hard for me because I wanted to be the best in what I was doing, so I studied a lot. Now, I know this helped me to understand that you should never stop learning and preparing yourself.

You might say I'm a bit of a firecracker. I move fast, talk fast, think fast, and I love my life.

SHIFTING FOCUS CHANGED MY LIFE
I have been involved with my church for almost 20 years

and play an active role in community service, mission trips, and in a multitude of small ways as well. Even with all of that, I was so busy in my corporate world, with all the responsibilities and travel, that it seemed to leave little time for anything else. Then Covid happened in March of 2020. I stopped traveling, and everything came to a screeching halt. That pause was exactly what I needed, even if I didn't realize it until it happened. It gave me time to think, look around me, and start looking for more ways to help others. It was at that time that servant leadership became more than an idea. It turned into my true focus; from there, so many doors opened and changed my life.

I asked myself, what else can I do? Is there a different path for me? Is there more? It was then that I became involved with a community organization. Once I got started and met new people, doors started opening. These gave me more opportunities to be the servant leader I knew in my heart that I was being called to. Those opportunities changed my life. It is a completely different world that I didn't see because I was focused on one thing—my job—and I never looked to the side.

Since then, other doors have opened that led me to become involved with Latina Empire, NAWBO, and other organizations that empower women. I also discovered I could mentor students, so I'm doing that through HISPA and loving every minute.

There are always special people in your life who influence you along the way. One of those in my life has been Jacqueline Camacho-Ruiz. She asked me, "What are you dreaming of?" When I answered, writing a book, she asked, "What are you waiting for? This is your moment." She gave me the tools to become a published author.

Another woman I admire is Maria Cortez, the executive director at my church. She has been a role model for me and my spiritual guide. Veronica Sosa showed me that I can have female friends with the same vision, through her organization of Sociedad Hispanas Emprendedoras (SHE), and of course Perla Tamez, founder of The Latina Empire, has been an inspiration both personally and in business, and I feel blessed to be her friend.

EMBARKING ON THE PATH OF SERVANT LEADERSHIP

Before embarking on my servant leadership journey, I focused on my career and being a leader. I was dedicating all my time to climbing the corporate ladder, becoming a part of our company management, and then becoming the director of the department. I love a challenge, so when work presented me with an opportunity to move to a completely different group, I took it. This move meant starting over as a manager and earning the director position a second time. I was always looking for leadership roles and forgot the part about being a servant.

For me, part of being a successful leader meant working on weekends, working while on vacation, always answering the phone, and constantly answering emails. It consumed my life and what should have been my free time, but the worst thing was I didn't realize what was happening. For me, it was normal if you wanted to hold those positions, if you wanted to be successful.

I guess you could say that my eyes started opening, and I started taking baby steps toward a change in 2019, with the biggest transformation, fully into servant leadership, when Covid hit in 2020. I began dedicating more time to myself, my family, and to everything else outside of work. When it came to changing my focus to servant leadership at work, that was easy because I'm a good listener, I'm persuasive, and I have the ability to get people to work together with me and achieve the goals we set.

It was difficult to accept when I realized how much time I had spent working instead of spending it with my family, of not doing things with my kids because I was busy with work or traveling. It was like someone lifted away a veil that had been in front of my eyes, and I thought, "What was I doing?" However, I don't think of it as a waste of time. I think you learn something from every journey you embark upon, and I think God allows you to live through certain things to learn from those situations.

In the end, I accomplished everything I wanted to, but I didn't realize the price I was paying for it. It was bittersweet because, on the one hand, I could be proud of those accomplishments, and it hurt my heart a bit due to the sacrifices.

GROWING, CONNECTING, REWARDING

If Covid hadn't happened and forced me to pause, I sometimes wonder how long it would have taken me to jump into the next phase of my life, to grow into servant leadership, and to build the incredible connections I have today. One of those was the National Association of Woman Business Owners

(NAWBO), a suggestion from Jaqueline Camacho two years ago, and now I'm president of the New Jersey chapter.

There is no question that I spend a significant amount of time helping others, whether through my church or one of the other organizations I'm connected to. But the reason why I do this is simple. It's rewarding. I feel good about helping people because I know I've helped to make a difference in someone's life. I'll never forget when, at the end of 2020, we were able, through the Hispanic Start NJ Hub where I was the leader, to pay the rent for some small business owners. We didn't know them, but the smiles and genuine gratitude from them gave me the best feeling you can get. When you know you've impacted someone's life in a significant way, there is no better feeling.

When I think about going through this process of change, of simplifying my life, I remember talking to a friend. She asked how I could get involved in so many different organizations and was a bit critical. I began explaining what I was doing, how I was doing it, and why. I explained the difference between a paycheck for a job done and changing people's lives. It was the first time my friend had heard that, and she realized she needed to join and get involved as well. She is now changing the lives of others as well. This is the ripple effect, which lets me have even more impact through people I am able to connect with others.

NAWBO is a national organization for women business owners with chapters throughout the country and is a one-stop resource to propel women business owners into greater economic and social spheres of power. Latina Empire is a global movement for personal and business growth that uses holistic techniques. Their "recipe" is heart, mind, and money through love, empowerment, peace, and freedom.

There are many nationwide organizations with chapters in your area where you can join and help make a difference for others.

MISSION TRIPS, ANOTHER WAY TO HELP OTHERS

I have been able to go on mission trips through my church. My first mission trip was in 2006, when we went to Argentina to put a roof on a school. The last one I went on was in 2019, when we went to Puerto Rico to help build houses after Hurricane Maria.

When my church organized a mission trip to Argentina to rebuild the roof of a school, I was all in. I have to say that what happened next was pretty funny.

Imagine with me. I had my tools, grit, and determination, and I was ready for the busy days installing a new tile roof. The first day I discovered the rest of my team—all men—expected me to help them by passing the tools or cooking, not working on the roof. I couldn't help but laugh at that. I had no intention of cooking, and couldn't if I wanted to. It didn't take long for the rest of my team to see they'd misjudged me as I quickly climbed the ladder and learned how to install a tile roof.

When we went to Puerto Rico, I worked on the roof once again. They were looking for a volunteer, and I said, ok, I'll do it. They all gave me a funny look and then cheered me on with a

"Look at you go!" as I climbed the ladder. I was fearless. I also learned to run the electric wire inside the walls at the direction of an electrician.

Here at my home church, Evangel Church, we have a program, Service for Service, where they organize projects around the community, helping people with work in or around their homes. It could mean cleaning, repairing something in the home, landscaping, painting, or whatever they need help with. Once we moved all the things from the patio to the basement for winter. This was to help an elderly couple who could not do it themselves.

LOVING THE CHALLENGES

I have always loved a good challenge, which is just as strong in me today as it was when I was a kid. I need challenges to continue living, while my husband doesn't like change. With him, I learned how difficult it is for some people. I didn't realize that other people don't look at challenges or change like I do. Because of this, I've been studying how to present challenges to people so they can embrace them by looking at the good things instead of focusing on the bad. I consider myself a change agent. I know how to present a challenge to make it easier for people to accept. We always have to deal with change--in life, work, in everything. And the easier people accept it, the better it is for them.

IT'S ALL ABOUT SIMPLICITY

One thing I value, that I like to share with others, is the value of simplicity. When you start complicating your life, your daily process, and your work--complicating anything--you get lost. You get lost on the way, and you get stressed by all the extra steps and things you create. When things are complicated, you lose focus and visibility of your goal. So, the more simplicity you can embrace, the simpler you can make things, and everything else will become easier. It will be easier to achieve your goals, complete projects, and plan your future.

The goal is to simplify everything—your life, your schedule, your job, projects you take on, and the processes you use to cook, clean, fix the car, go for a promotion, or hire an employee. The simpler it is, the faster and easier you will see results. I am a certified Lean Six Sigma Master Black Belt. Six Sigma is a data-driven technique that encourages continuous improvement by focusing on flaws, inconsistencies, and waste elimination. Although, this is designed for business, you can use the same principles to simplify things in your own life.

To use these principles, answer these questions. What is your goal? What is your current situation? What steps do you need to take to reach your goal? It could be training, preparation, or tasks. Take small steps forward until you reach your goal. Too often, people will have a huge goal and try to go too far, too fast. The best way is to take a small step, reevaluate your situation, decide what the next small step should be, and take it. Then, continue the process until you reach your goal. For this process you can use the tool KATA. It's like going up the stairs. You take the first step and realize it is complete, so you can take the next step up and repeat it until you get to the top.

TRUST YOURSELF

When you make changes, there will always be people who tell you that you shouldn't do it, who say you're doing the wrong thing, who doubt you, or say that you will fail. Whatever you are working on, whether it's self-improvement, learning new technology, or becoming a servant leader, I believe you should trust yourself.

For me, I put everything in prayer first, and when I feel I know what God wants me to do, then that's what I do. I have so much confidence in God that it doesn't matter to me how difficult the situation is; I know he will get me to the other side. I know I need to prepare and do my part, but God has my back. Even with that, failure can be part of the process, and we need to learn something from it.

You should build your self-confidence and always be prepared to fail as that can be part of the learning process. Sometimes people don't do things because they're afraid to fail. They think the world will end if they fail, but it won't.

One of the biggest obstacles I have worked to overcome is my accent. People didn't understand me in English, Spanish, or any other language I tried. My mom and family would say I talked too fast in Spanish, while other people would say they don't understand me in English. I have worked hard on communication and failed many times--I had to repeat myself, slow down, and focus on my pronunciation. I think part of the problem is that my brain works really fast, and my mouth is trying to keep up. This is why I challenged myself and decided to obtain a certification as a speaker. Now that I have it, I am working on improving every day.

In the end, if you fail, it doesn't matter. You will never know if you can do something if you don't try. If you fail, stand up and try again. That's how people make the biggest achievements in their lives, by being willing to take chances and fail. Often things don't work out on the first try. Embrace failure as part of the learning process, and you won't just learn. You'll fly. You'll reach your goals. You'll have dreams come true.

ADVICE AND A CHALLENGE

If I could give any advice, it would be what I teach my kids and what I live by: God is in control of everything, we just need to ask for his direction. I would also encourage you to stop complicating your life, this is affecting your mental health and causing stress and anxiety.

I challenge you today to think about your day or week and discover how many processes you have in your life that you don't need, that no longer serve you. See how many ways you can simplify your life and then reap the reward of more time and energy to do the things that give you joy.

BIOGRAPHY

Adriana Rozo-Angulo is a passionate leader, strategist, and change agent who fervently believes that processes are a tool for growth, and business and personal success is possible in a simple and stress-free way. This is what she calls SIMPLICOLOGIA.

Adriana Rozo-Angulo is the President of MAS Connections, a business consultancy firm she co-found in 2011 and she is a Director of Operations at Menasha. Adriana is a certified Lean Six Sigma Master Black Belt professional and holds several certifications in the manufacturing and medical device industry.

Adriana is a certified EXMA speaker, author of THE BUOYANT BUSINESS and the Spanish version BAJO EL AGUA, and co-author of the books "Today's Inspired Latina IX" and "Hispanic Star Rising I". Adriana is also the president of NAWBO (National Association of Women Business Owners), NJ Chapter, a member of the Advisory Board of Seton Hall University for the "Transformative Leadership in Disruptive Times" executive certificate program, and the New Jersey chapter Leader for The Latina Empire.

Adriana Rozo-Angulo

www.adrianarozoangulo.com

LinkedIn: Adriana Rozo-Angulo

BECOME THE LEADER YOU ARE MEANT TO BE

America Baez

*"Don't wait to pursue your dreams. Go for it.
You can do anything you want."*

I've always had big dreams. They started when I was a child, living in a small town in Mexico. My parents were fueled by creativity, and they shared those talents and experiences with me, making my childhood wonderfully unique.

Both of my parents were teachers, politicians, and active in our community. They were also dancers, and my father is an artist, too. He's a songwriter and has published five books of poetry. My mom was the director for social services in our county and was the campaign manager for a politician in our town who won office twice.

They inspired me to follow my dreams, to be active, to explore my own creativity, my artistry, and as a result, I took sewing and cooking classes and got involved in sports. There wasn't anything I was discouraged from trying, and my parents worked hard to provide me with whatever I needed.

I also learned to see the value in fostering connections through the example my parents set because they knew almost everyone in town. Although my parents were very strict and protective of me, they supported and encouraged me to discover my own interests and passion.

When I was about 12 years old, I began thinking about moving somewhere else and being exposed to other things. I had seen a lot of different places, different countries and cities on TV, and thought the world was so big I needed to go out and see it.

It was a thought that, over time, became a goal that drove much of what I did.

FUELED BY DETERMINATION

While I was in college, that desire grew to see what was out there beyond the country I lived in. I decided to learn English because it's the world's language. I didn't yet know how I was going to use it or what I planned to do with it, but I had to learn it.

Once I graduated, I started working at the local bank. Eventually, I earned a vacation from work, and I told my dad that I wanted to visit the United States, not just the border where we would go shopping.

I would ask, "Do we know anybody living in the United States?" He would say, "No, no, we don't," and I kept questioning him because I thought everyone had some family there. But he kept saying no.

As it turned out, it was my mom who, after several days of persistent questioning on my part, gave in. She said we had family in Chicago and had bumped into them six months earlier when they were back in Mexico for a visit.

Several days more went by as I begged my parents to call our family in Chicago to see if I could visit. I finally realized they weren't going to do that, so one day when my dad wasn't home, I got the phone number from my mom.

I was determined to go, so I immediately called the number I'd been given. It was a grown man who answered, and I launched into an explanation of who I was, how we were related, and asked if I could come to visit as I wanted to see Chicago. He agreed, and it was at that moment my American adventure began.

THE ADVENTURE BEGINS

I was 23 and very excited to be reaching the goal I'd had as a child—to travel and discover what life was like in other places, starting with Chicago, known as the Windy City, and sitting on the southern end of Lake Michigan.

First, though, I had to get ready, and that meant renewing my passport and visa, as both had expired. Renewing my passport was easily done in a nearby city, and I went there the next day. Renewing my visa, however, required that I travel to the border, something that I didn't want to do alone.

I asked my dad to go with me, and he said he was too busy and that he had things to do. So, I went by myself. I was a little nervous but took the bus at 5 a.m. for the four-hour ride to the border, hopped in a taxi, and made it to the consulate. The return trip was uneventful but made for a long day.

The next day, I notified the bank that I would be taking vacation time, and within a week after calling my cousin, I was traveling to Chicago by bus. I didn't speak English at the time, but I could read a little.

I got to the bus station in Chicago and called my cousin. It wasn't long before this guy with a beard, ponytail, tattoos, and wearing shorts, came up to me and said, "Hi America, I'm Charlie. My mom is out in the car." I was a bit of a surprise for them, too, because they thought I'd come in a few months, not a week later.

I hit it off with my cousins, and when I told them I wanted to study English, they told me I could come back to Chicago and stay with them for a while. That way, I could attend ESL classes at one of the colleges in Chicago.

I didn't waste any time. Once I returned home, I worked and saved my money with plans to go back to Chicago in six months. Four months later, something happened that could have ended all my plans, but I was determined that nothing would stand in my way.

I HAVE WHAT?

Two months before I planned to return to Chicago, I was diagnosed with a brain tumor. It was discovered early, and I had to undergo a lot of tests and an MRI. Then my doctor gave me the diagnosis, and I asked him what I needed to do to take care of it because I had plans. I was leaving for the United States in two months.

We agreed on treatment and made a plan. Then I went home and told my parents that I was moving to Chicago in two months, and, by the way, I have a brain tumor. Of course, my parents didn't want me to go.

I couldn't let anything get in the way of my dreams and plans for the future, so I sold my car, quit my job two months later, and then I was back in Chicago, ready to take classes. I lived with my cousins for a few months before finding a very small apartment where I could afford to live on my own.

I had to return to Mexico to see my doctor every few months for check-ups and medication. Treatment took six years, and I gratefully went into remission in 2000. While I was going through treatment, I didn't tell anyone that I had a brain tumor because it changes how people look at you.

Even though it's in remission, I still take medication and get tested from time to time because there are no guarantees that it won't come back.

THE NEXT PHASE: PROFESSIONAL GROWTH

After 18 months, I finished the English program and returned to Mexico, where I got a job working for the government. Then, I decided I was ready to move to Texas, so I could earn my MBA, and a year later returned to Chicago looking for a job.

It was 2000 when I joined Prospanica, the National Society of Hispanic MBAs, and in 2001 I began volunteering, attending events, and networking in Chicago as I continued my job search. I loved being involved and even became the chapter president 3-4 years later.

My passion for diving in and making a difference also took me on a leadership journey. I knew that this path was meant for me, and it helped me to grow personally and professionally. We did a lot of great things and in two years, grew the membership by 70 percent.

I was elected to the Prospanica national board and years later I won Prospanica's National Brillante Award. I credit my career to that organization because that's when I started meeting people and developing personally and professionally.

FROM SEEKING EMPLOYMENT TO GIVING BACK

Employment is a challenge for just about everyone at one time or another, especially in today's work environment. After returning to Chicago, it took me a year to find a job.

This was because I came to the US as an international student, and that meant I had to find a company to sponsor my work visa. I got a couple of offers that were rescinded because they decided they didn't want to deal with the requirements surrounding the sponsorship.

It was a very stressful time, but I eventually landed an IT project administrator job with a small consulting company in Chicago. I worked with their client, a large insurance company, at their headquarters and supported their project managers. It was a great experience to be in that environment, in corporate America, and to be exposed to so much.

I stayed there for three-and-a-half years. I was already involved with Prospanica, and I became the Chicago Chapter President around that time. I was meeting new people but, more importantly, I was channeling my creativity and enjoying giving back to my community.

I really believed, and I still do, in the mission to provide professional development programs and give members access to companies. They had a lot of programs, from professional development to partnerships with different companies that wanted to hire our members. We also did all kinds of events, from conferences and networking to career fairs, and fundraising for scholarships.

I did that for years and got very little sleep.

HELPING PEOPLE IN A DIFFERENT WAY

One of the many reasons I love Prospanica is the opportunity it has given me to lift up others. I suppose it was only natural that others there liked to do the same thing, and sometimes it happened quietly during a conversation exchanging meaningful information.

I was at another successful event, networking as usual, when I had a conversation with a man who, at that time, was VP of HR at a big company. He asked me if I would consider a job in HR and recruiting.

I hadn't ever thought about it but ended up agreeing to an interview. I was offered the job and have stayed in that field ever since (more than 15 years). I advanced with each job I've taken since that time, first at Comcast, Pepsi, then U.S. Cellular, Baxter, Accenture, and, most recently, Verizon for the last five years.

Because I was in recruiting, I was always bringing diversity and inclusion into the conversation with my employers. I would explain that there's an opportunity for us to do more in that space, and I happened to be involved with this organization. Could we explore a partnership or something? The companies were receptive and supportive, so I would develop partnerships with them and other diverse non-Hispanic organizations.

I was working on diversity and inclusion, even back then when it wasn't a thing like it is today. So, I did that in different capacities throughout my career. At Verizon, my last job, which I just left a couple of months ago, that's where it was more focused on diversity, equity, and inclusion, especially in the last three years.

As the head of diversity and inclusion talent acquisition programs, I created the diversity recruiting strategy, and I led the operations for the entire company. When I started working at Verizon, I was a senior manager in talent acquisition programs, and I was also working on campus recruiting, internships and employment branding. And then, after two years, I moved to a corporate role where I built the diverse talent pipeline for the entire company.

It feels as though I've come full circle. Twenty-two years ago, when I joined Prospanica, I didn't know anybody. I was just another member. Now, after a long journey and a lot of challenges, I've been heading diversity and inclusion recruiting programs for Verizon, a top company, and I'm sponsoring the organization. I'm the one coordinating Verizon's participation in their conference, as well as many others.

I have several philosophies, and one is if there is a will, there's a way. Another is you have to think big. I think big. I cannot think small. I told my Prospanica Chicago chapter board, the first day I was the chapter president, we have to think big. We're not going to think about all the things that we don't have--we don't have volunteers, we don't have money, we don't have sponsors, etc. No, we're going to think about how we want to position the chapter and the organization in the city and around the country compared to the other chapters. And then, we make a plan for marketing, membership, sponsorships, volunteers we create committees. Then we execute. And that's what we did. We were very, very successful. That's just how I operate.

THE ROAD AHEAD

Another important part of my life is I have faith. I have faith that things will happen. I know that when you take a step, and you reach that goal, then you look to see what the next step is that you need to take toward your goals. A step at a time. Obviously, as time goes by, there are other goals.

Today is a good example. I've left Verizon, and I'm thinking, what am I going to do in the next five or 10 years? Sometimes that is not very clear. It may be more so now because I have more experience. It wasn't clear when I was younger, but I knew there were other things that I wanted to do.

When I was a new member of Prospanica 20 years ago, and I would see all these women speaking at a conference, that was a huge deal for me. I thought, wow. I would like to get invited and have the presence to do that. I didn't know when or how, but why not? I could do it, and now I do.

I've been exposed to a lot of things, and now I feel more confident, too.

A VISIONARY INSPIRES OTHERS

Both of my parents had a huge influence on me, but the biggest influence was my dad, especially early on. He still is, with his books of poetry. Before he wrote the books, he'd always loved writing and was writing things, but never a full book.

He was getting invited to all these cities around the country, and to festivals to present the book and his poetry. He's living his best life, and then he wrote a second book, a third book, and he did that all by himself. And so, it's things like that, they would tell me all these amazing things, and I'm so proud of them.

Over the years, as I saw more of what my mom did, I realized how amazing she was. I would get calls to catch up, and they would say how some candidate wanted to meet with my mom and asked her to be his campaign manager, just like that. And now she has started organizing this and coordinating all these projects and leading people. She was fearless, and she just got things done. That's where I got it from.

Just as my parents inspired me, I hope to do that for others. One of my strengths that emerged a long time ago and was confirmed when I took the Gallup Strength Finder survey, is that I am a natural futuristic or visionary. When I read the description I thought, they're reading my soul right here.

Obviously, being a visionary is about having a vision of the things that can or should be, but the idea is that you're always thinking ahead to what's beyond the horizon. There is no little idea. What really caught my attention was when it said you inspire people, and they can follow your lead. People with those visionary skills can also practice being better at it.

A FEW BITS OF ADVICE

I think being resilient and having grit—sticking to what you believe in—is important. Even more, don't wait to do something. Don't wait to pursue your dreams. Go for it. You can do anything you want.

Don't be afraid to fail. When pursuing your goals, it may turn out ok, or it may not, but you'll never know if you don't try. And if you fall? Get right back up and try again. Keep trying until you find success.

My sister died from stage four breast cancer, and after the grief and stress, trying to climb out of that black hole, I feel like a different person. It has emphasized how short life can be and how anything can happen. So don't wait on your dreams. There are no guarantees.

It's also crucial for you to be genuine and authentic. That's how I live my life. Everything that I go after is always with the best intention. I've been involved with so many organizations in leadership positions, giving back to the communities for more than 15 years. That is my life mission. I want to elevate people.

To help you take the next step, answer these few questions. What is your life mission? What gives your life meaning? What are your dreams and goals? Once you've answered them, go out there and become the leader you are meant to be.

BIOGRAPHY

America Baez has an extensive career as a global thought leader in talent acquisition and diversity, equity & inclusion. She has implemented transformational global DEI talent solutions for Fortune 100 companies including Accenture, Comcast and most recently led the global diversity recruiting operations strategy for Verizon.

America has held leadership roles in several organizations including Prospanica (formerly known as NSHMBA) where she was Chicago chapter president and national board member. She has also served in the Society of Talent Acquisition & Recruitment (STAR Chicago) board for several years where she launched the first-ever mentoring program for recruiting professionals. Recent accolades include the "2020 Diversity MBA Top 100 Emerging Leaders" award, "Who's Who" in Hispanic Business in Chicago by Negocios Now, and the prestigious Prospanica National "Brillante" Award, just to name a few.

America was selected as a National Hispana Leadership Institute (NHLI) Executive Leadership Program Fellow and invited by the We Are All Human organization to be a Hispanic STAR Ambassador. She completed leadership development programs at Harvard University and the Center for Creative Leadership (CCL) in Portugal.

She earned her MBA from Texas A&M International University and a Directorship Certification from the National Association of Corporate Directors (NACD). In her free time, she enjoys mentoring professionals and allowing them to discover their true genius and spending time with family.

America Baez
Twitter: @AmericaBaez
LinkedIn: America Baez

NAVIGATING LEADERSHIP WITH PURPOSE AND INTENTION

Dr. Anitza San Miguel

"Navigate in peace in the direction of your dream. Stay focused, trust, believe and take action."

As I reflect on my leadership journey, I can´t stop thinking about my upbringing, how much I have grown, and how many people have impacted my life. I am a leader not by chance, but by purpose, intention, and calling. I know these three words sometimes don´t go along with leadership, but today I can confidently say that those three words summarize my leadership journey over the last three years.

I grew up in Toa Baja, Puerto Rico, also known as *la Isla del Encanto* (the Island of Enchantment) surrounded by family and friends who always saw something in me. I was the overachiever of the family. My family was imperfectly perfect as many families. Both of my parents didn't go to college, but they knew the value of education and of obtaining a degree to be alguien en la vida (someone in life).

My dad had the opportunity to attend a junior college in New York City. He even received a scholarship. But he never attended college nor did he take advantage of the scholarship. When I found out about this, I was in shock. I suddenly felt this urge to ask why not? I wanted to know what happened. I felt I deserved to know. But it was too late. I found out about it when my mom, brother, and I were going through my dad's personal belonging days after he passed away. I wished I had known earlier, so I could ask him why he didn't attend college. Clearly, he had the potential. I sometimes wondered what he would have accomplished if he had gone to college. Perhaps, his view of leadership would have been different. My dad worked at American Airlines in the cargo division. He had the opportunity to take on a leadership role. I remembered asking him why he didn't go into management. His response, *"No quiero ese dolor the cabeza"* (I don't want that headache). Years later, as I faced my own headaches in leadership, I understood why he didn't want the headache.

My mom also knew the value of education. She worked as a secretary (now called administrative assistant) at a law office in Puerto Rico. She saw firsthand how much the attorneys had to prepare to be the best in the field of mortgage law. Their education opened doors for them, and she wanted that for me and my brother. To excel. To have a title. To have a degree. To be someone. As for me, I learned so much from each of the attorneys at the firm as each of them had a unique leadership style.

I worked during the summers at the law office, so I got firsthand experience on what I thought leadership looked like. While my friends were enjoying their summers doing fun extracurricular activities, going to the beach, and traveling, I was working at the office. I have no regrets. I learned so much about what I could do in life. At some point, I wanted to be an attorney. But, after working at the office, I didn't see myself dealing with different client issues, going to court, and dealing with the stress.

I took my first leadership steps at a small church in my hometown Toa Baja. During my teenage years, I volunteered as a Sunday school teacher and at summer camps. My memories of this time are vague. No one trained me to be a Sunday school teacher. I just did it. I stepped up to the plate to help the church leaders teach the next generation.

Thirty years later, I can confidently say that those experiences started developing me as a leader. Little did I know that I would be where I am today and I'm proud of my journey.

IS IT LONELY AT THE TOP?

When I started my leadership journey in education twenty years ago, I didn't know what I was getting into. You would think

I would know, but I didn't. I started navigating education first as a part-time faculty, then full-time faculty, moving to assistant dean, interim associate dean, and finally dean of science. For some, it seemed to be too fast. I was too young to be in a position of leadership. For me, it felt normal. However, deep inside, I was lost.

I remember one of my colleagues tell me, "Anitza, as you go higher up the ladder, it gets lonely." I believed it. I felt lonely so many times as I was starting to navigate not only leadership but leadership in higher education. Almost nine years ago, I felt I couldn't trust anyone. I felt that the world in higher education was against me. I felt I was a failure. I doubted my skills and abilities. I questioned many times why I was doing what I was doing. At one point, there was so much negativity and power struggle around me that I couldn't stand it. There were many times that I cried on my way home from work and other times I cried myself to sleep without my husband knowing my struggle. My dream of going up the ladder and breaking the famous glass ceiling kept me going. However, I started having doubts. Is this what I really want? Am I pursuing a career because this is what I want or because I am living someone else's dream?

One of the first leadership programs in higher education I participated in was the National Community College Hispanic Council (NCCHC) Leadership Fellows Program. It was in this program that I realized that I was not alone. I realized that there were other administrators having the same challenges. They all were navigating different issues. I thought to myself, I found my tribe!

I also remember attending a breakfast at the National Library of Congress in Washington, DC, sponsored by the National Hispana Leadership Institute (NHLI). I met so many amazing Latinas from different professions, countries, and walks of life. I told myself, I want to participate in the NHLI program, but immediately I felt I was unqualified. I felt I didn't have the experience to back me up. So, I waited almost six years before I applied to the program. In 2014, I participated in the NHLI. This was one of the best leadership programs as its purpose was to address the lack of representation of Latinas in leadership positions. There, I met and gained sixteen amazing *"hermanas"* (my sisters). It was with these women that I started to build my confidence.

I remember sharing with one of our speakers at the NHLI program the challenges I was having at work and how I was doubting myself. She looked me in the eyes and very calmly said, "Anitza, it is not you. You have outgrown the place. It's time to move." My first thought was, "Is she crazy? I am not moving!" A woman with a vision and purpose, helping other Latinas, she was right. For me to move to the next level, I had to navigate new waters. Two years later, I moved to Orlando, Florida.

It was just three years ago that I discovered I could have an inner circle that I could trust. You are probably wondering, "What's an inner circle?" An inner circle is a close group of colleagues, family, and friends (five or six, for example) that you can trust. Think about it as your executive board. These are people who deeply, authentically, and genuinely care for you and your well-being. These are people who see your potential. The people who will tell you when you are going in the opposite direction. Those are the people who will support you. It was three years ago, when I started forming my inner circle. Early in my leadership journey, I only trusted two to three individuals. Why? Because those who I thought had my back did not and I learned to be careful. I also learned to protect my dreams. There are a lot of dream robbers out there.

WHO AM I?

That's the question I asked myself three years ago. If I leave my job today, who am I?

As leaders, we sometimes allow our work or job to define who we are and that must not be the case. So many people lose sight of who they are. I was one of them! For so many years, I focused on my career and my job title defined who I was. When people asked me, "What do you do?" my immediate response was, "I am a dean of science." Well, when I started my intentional growth journey, I learned that is not what I do. That's my occupation. Now, my response is, "I help leaders reignite their potential through the renewal of their mind so they can create a new story."

It was during the pandemic that I felt I was called to do more, to be more, to have a broader impact, and to lead more intentionally. I realized I had lost sight of who I was, my purpose, and my calling. See, when God calls you, he will equip you and it takes time. I feel I have been in a season of waiting. It is so hard to wait for something. But everything has its time and place.

There is a big difference between what I do and who I am. I work as a dean in a higher education institution. Who am I? I am an author, speaker, a woman of faith, scientist, educator, mentor, coach, mother, wife, and so much more.

WHY DON'T YOU SPEAK UP?

Earlier in my career and up to three years ago (yes, three years ago!), I used to be quiet in meetings and other venues. I would share or say just what I needed or because it was my turn to give an update. This is what some introverts do. Why? I didn't want to cause trouble or create chaos. Early in my life, I was taught by my parents, *"Calladita te ves más bonita"* or *"Que va a decir la gente"* (You look pretty when you are quiet or What will people say)." So, I didn't speak my mind. I would come home from work and share with my husband something that had happened at work and how annoyed I was about it. His first response, "Did you say anything?" Silence. He will go on to ask me why and he will go nonstop about how I needed to be more vocal.

Early in our marriage, my husband used to also tell me, that he noticed that we would go to events or parties and that I was too quiet. He just told me, "Anitza, people don't even notice that you were at the party." His observations and comments annoyed me so much. I was not him, an extrovert. I am an introvert and he (and everyone else) had to accept me as I am. I was so wrong! After this realization, I started to network more (intentionally) and to speak up.

Every time I had to speak up at a meeting, I always felt a rush in my body. My hands and armpits would start sweating. The struggle was real for me. I remember one time in a meeting, I overheard one of my colleagues say, "Why is she not speaking up?" It suddenly clicked. I need to start navigating leadership in a different way. I must be and do me and not what others want me to be. I need to let myself loose. I needed to let the bird out of the cage and allow it to fly in the friendly skies with confidence.

Three years later (yes, it took me all these years), I said to myself, *"You can't keep doing this. Your voice needs to be heard. You not only have a seat at the table, but also a voice at the table."* I now have finally started navigating in the direction of my dreams and goals. I started to trust and believe in me!

WHAT HAVE I LEARNED?

Leadership with purpose, intention, and calling is a journey. It's a journey that only you decide to embark on. There have been days in my career that I have questioned myself. I have questioned my leadership skills. Days of doubt and fear of failure have invaded my soul and, at times, have paralyzed me. But, three years ago I left the comfort zone. I decided to set sail on an amazing journey that has transformed me into a better person and leader. Since the day I started my career in science and later in education, I knew there was always something else for me out there. There were times where I felt like a bird inside a cage. A bird that had outgrown their cage and needed a new one but, for some reason, didn't get one. That cage was so small that the limiting beliefs about my leadership skills were constantly reminding me that I was not good enough. Have you had that feeling? That feeling of anxiety where your chest gets super tight because you know deep in your heart that there is something better for you.

The day I decided to set sail into my intentional growth journey, that was the day that I started reigniting my potential. That was the day the bird opened the door and saw, at a distance, the light. It has been three years of growth and development as an individual. I attribute my passion of helping leaders reignite their potential and transform their life to my own experiences of renewing my mind and to the work I have done to move outside the comfort zone. So, how did I do it? Three very simple strategies:

1. **Prepare:** You must prepare. When you go on vacation, what do you do? You prepare. You find and reserve your hotel, car, tours, and airline tickets. The same goes for us as leaders. Do you want to be a better leader? Do you want a promotion? Do you want to start a business? I have three words for you: prepare, listen, act. I cannot give to others what I don't have. I must prepare to help them develop. I must prepare to inspire them. I must nurture my soul so I can help them unleash their potential. Preparation is everything.

2. **Listen:** You must learn to listen carefully. Pay close attention to what your people are telling you. What is the essence of the issue? How are they feeling? Ask questions. Be curious. I have learned that sometimes

people just want to be heard. They want someone who can listen to them without judgement. As leaders, we must learn to listen. We also need to learn to listen to our intuition. My intuition never fails. Learn to discern when your intuition is talking to you. It is that nudge that makes you uncomfortable. Listen! It's nudging you for a reason.

3. **Act:** Without action, nothing happens. If I had not decided to embark on my intentional growth journey and taken action, I would not be writing this story. Action propels me to be at another level. Action propelled me to share my story with others, because my voice needs to be heard. My story matters. My Latino community needs me.

I now see leadership as a learning process. I have learned from each of my failure and rejection moments. No one likes pain. If leadership were pain free, the world would be a better place. As I share with you my story, I feel free. The bird is out of the cage! The bird is free to fly in the sky. That bird is me.

LOOKING INTO THE FUTURE

Today, I lead with intention and purpose. As my mentor John Maxwell says, "People don't care how much you know until they know how much you care." This is so true. I can have all the titles in the world; but if I don't care about the people I serve, the people I lead, then my leadership is not authentic and real. As a leader, all it takes is a message, a word of encouragement to our team.

As I continue my leadership journey, I commit to keep on growing. Yes! Personal growth and development doesn't stop when you obtain a leadership title, promotion, or new job. Personal growth and development are continuous. The moment I stop growing, I die. As leaders, we need to keep learning about ourselves. I invite you to take time to reflect on your leadership journey. Where are you now? Where were you last year? Where are you going? These are three key questions that I reflect on every couple of months as they help me to assess my growth.

I now navigate with purpose and intention. I navigate in the direction of my dreams and goals. I navigate in peace knowing that God is in control. In every challenge I face, there is a teaching moment. Every challenge prepares me for something bigger and better. I am in this world for a reason. You are in this world for a reason. You have a purpose. Navigate in your purpose. Navigate in your calling.

REFLECTION QUESTIONS

In your journal, reflect and answer the following questions:

1. What is your purpose?
2. How has your leadership journey shaped you?
3. What can you do as a leader to help others in your team to grow and to develop?
4. Why do some individuals dislike being in a leadership role?

BIOGRAPHY

Dr. Anitza San Miguel is scientist, educator, and transformational leadership mentor. Her purpose is to help leaders transform their mind and unleash their potential to create their best version without limits.

Her passion for personal growth and development drives her to grow daily. She has more than 20 years of experience in research and education. She has served as a science professor and Dean of Science at institutions in Virginia and Florida, and currently serves as a dean leading a team in the Orlando, Florida area. She worked at the National Institutes of Health (NIH) and the United States Patent and Trademark Office (USPTO).

She is also the founder of ASM Mentors, creator of the podcast "Sacúdete y Toma Acción" translated in English as "Shake It Off and Take Action". Dr. San Miguel has been showcased in numerous platforms in social media, and other events, including TV programs in Puerto Rico. She authored Navegador, a reflective journaling tool with reflection cards, and featured as an insightful author in Today´s Inspired Latina Volume X book series. A sought-out speaker, mentor and coach.

Dr. San Miguel firmly believes that everything is possible if you trust, believe, and take action. Her attitude, positive energy, and determination have led her to achieve her professional and personal goals.

When she's not working, you'll find her spending quality time with her husband and 13-year-old daughter, traveling, and journaling.

She is passionate about education that leads to the academic and professional success of leaders with the mission of discovering their best version without limits.

Dr. Anitza San Miguel
anitza@anitzasanmiguel.com
LinkedIn: /anitza-sanmiguel
IG: @anitza21

DEVELOPING LEADERSHIP ONE STEP AT A TIME

―

Araceli Zanabria

"Resilience is the greatest of my attributes."

No matter how difficult the challenges are that I face in life, I know that I will be able to stand up straight and face them directly. I know that I will be able to overcome them, even if they are painful and require me to reinvent myself.

I am not afraid to change. However, I have high standards, and although it may not come as quickly as I want sometimes, I am determined to overcome whatever is put before me and have a positive outcome.

I was made like the palm trees that bend but do not break during a hurricane. They may lose some fronds, but those will grow back in time. I have learned that I am resilient and that when my hurricane arrives, I will bend to the wind and come out of it as a survivor.

A HUNGER TO LEARN

I am the second of 10 children—nine daughters and one son. We grew up in Mexico, and my parents were old school. I was always curious when I was little, and I wanted to learn about everything. If my mom was cooking or sewing, I wanted to know how to do it, too.

I was hungry to learn, and as I have gone through life, this quest for knowledge has resulted in many experiences I might not have had otherwise. One of those experiences was when I was awarded a scholarship during my middle school years.

As I continued through high school and was getting ready for college, I faced more challenges because I chose to be different. I was interested in become an agronomist engineer, a traditionally male-dominated field.

This was my true passion at that time, but I had to fight with my father, too, before he could see what it meant to me. He thought it wasn't a career for women, that it was too hard and required too much heavy work. He might have thought I was being a bit rebellious, but I knew I could do it. Hard work does not scare me, and I knew in my heart that I would be successful.

It didn't matter to me, though, and even though it was hard, I did it. I graduated from college with a degree in agronomist engineering. I accomplished this by attending school full-time, working part-time, and keeping my grades high.

I learned that I'm strong, I know what I want, and I can do anything I set my mind on. All I have to do is decide on a goal and go for it. This philosophy worked well for me throughout the years, especially when I came to the United States in 1988, a year after I graduated.

PLANS CHANGE QUICKLY

I decided to come to United the States for 12 months to earn some money and go back home to get my career started. The goal was to work as an agronomist engineer in an institution and be an entrepreneur by opening a fertilizer store because I knew how hard it would be to save money working in a regular job.

As will happen when life gets in the way, things change. Instead of achieving what I had planned, I met my children's father, now my ex-husband, and I got pregnant with our first son, Benny. He was born with cerebral Palsy, so I entered the world of special needs children.

We also had a second child, Irving, and I was devoted to our children. Benny gave me the strength to be better every day and motivated me to do whatever it took to give him a better life. And I did it until the last day of his life, just before he turned 18. It was a miracle to have him with us for that long because the doctors had told us he would only live to be five or six years old, but my ex-husband and I worked together, and we did a good job, taking very good care of him. When Benny died in 2007, I struggled and spent the next six years in the dark, grieving.

Then, in 2011, our younger son, Irving, was diagnosed with

TODAY'S INSPIRED LEADER VOLUME IV

cancer, and that just took me down further. But Irving reminded me that Benny had been so happy, even though he had no hope of getting better and endured much pain. He told me, "Mom, I'm going to be ok."

He was right. Today, he is a cancer survivor, overcoming everything, including surgery and chemo. Even though it took him down and made him tired, he still went to school. He might have to be picked up early, but he went.

I love his attitude, and he was the one who helped me finally get past Benny's death. He told me I needed to let Benny go, and even though it was hard, I was able to do that.

Today, Irving remains cancer free and is 28 years old. He graduated from college, and I am proud of the man he's become. Combining my work and life as a mother has helped me grow into the best version of myself.

PUTTING MY CHILDREN'S NEEDS FIRST

My father, Jose Luis Sanabria, has been the example, the leader, in my life. He was strong, independent, and hardworking. I inherited many of his personality traits. He always told me that if I knew how to do things, I would be a good boss, and I had to tell people who worked for me how to do the work if it wasn't done right.

Even though I see myself as very similar to my father, there are some things that I want to do differently because I didn't agree with the way he did them. So, while I am developing many of the traits we have in common, I also do my best to be different.

Benny is the reason I am established here. I had to make sure I could pay for the best doctors, hospitals, insurance, and surgeries. I worked 12 hours a day, seven days a week, for at least five years to make sure I could provide my children with the best.

Today, I am a real estate broker and will celebrate 21 years in this business in January 2023. I am also a real estate investor, something I have done for the last 18 years.

After 3 years working as a Realtor, I decided to invest my savings in real estate in the United States. I built a home in Mexico because I wanted to move back home, but the situation was not easy there for a child with special needs.

BECOMING A REAL ESTATE BROKER

There came a point when I said to myself, "I've got move on to a different level." I was learning English, and I met an agent who was a real estate broker.

I asked him, "Can I work with you? In the office, I want to learn and could be your apprentice." He said ok even though I only spoke about 50 percent English, but I knew myself. If I want to do something, I will make it happen, regardless of any obstacles. He needed someone to work in the office every day, and I only lived 10 blocks away.

He agreed to let me work in his office, and when I decided to take my first real estate class, he offered to pay for it. I told him no because I wanted to make myself proud by getting my license on my own merit.

I used the money I earned from the first rental I arranged

to pay for the class and attended night sessions three days a week. At the end of the course, I had to take the class test before I could take the state exam to be licensed.

The instructor doubted I would pass because I was so quiet and said very little--my English didn't allow me to have conversations. Our test was on Wednesday, and the state exam was the following Tuesday. When I went to class on Friday to get the test results, he handed me my graded test. It showed I'd gotten a 95 and had a smiley face next to it. He wished me the best and said he knew I would make it happen.

I also passed the state exam on the first try the following week. While others had doubts because of the language barrier, I always knew that I would pass.

Becoming a real estate broker was just an opportunity that I saw, it has become my true passion and has been very rewarding. I save money over the years and invest in Real Estate.

STARTING MY OWN BUSINESS

To become a real estate broker, you must earn a certain number of sales & points. In other words, to have a certain level of experience. I was able to earn all that I needed within the first year, and exactly a year after I took my first class, I was able to get my broker's license.

It was not an easy thing to do because there was a time during that year when I was racing from work to home to the hospital because Benny had back surgery. My husband and I worked together so that Benny always had someone there, and after he recovered, I made it to my goal.

If I want to do something, I prepare, I study, and I'm very structured about how I achieve my goals and overcome challenges. A lot of people see me as very regimented and strict, but I'm just very organized, and I don't like to do things more than once if I don't have to.

This part of my personality has helped me throughout my life and has been instrumental in helping me become a leader who is trusted by those she leads. The agents who have worked in my brokerage know that I require just as much of myself as I do for them.

I enjoy educating the consumer as well so that the process of buying and selling their property is not stressful. It is very rewarding when I can help so many families become homeowners and fulfill the American dream.

I provide honest and ethical service to my clients. Doing this makes an impression on my clients, and they respond by referring my services and bringing me repeat business.

I love working in real estate because seeing the smiles when people buy their dream home makes me feel like I'm getting my own dream home every time. It fills my heart.

I learned I could do anything when my father got sick when I was 14. Life was hard. My siblings and I no longer had a home where we belonged, and we bounced from one home to another before going to live at my grandmom's. There were a lot of needs to cover and I ended up taking over my father's business making flautas.

I would get up very early to prepare everything for the

flautas before I ran—literally—for 30 minutes to get to school in time. I would be sweating like crazy by the time I got there. I worked after school, too, and I was able to earn enough to pay for the food we needed, supplies for school, clothes, and shoes.

That experience marked my life and was the reason I knew I could do anything I decided I wanted to do, including opening my own business so many years later.

GIVING BACK THROUGH MAKE-A-WISH FOUNDATION

The Make-A-Wish Foundation grants wishes to children who are facing critical illness. They say, "When a wish comes true, it creates strength, hope, and transformation in a child and a community."

I know that being a leader isn't limited to business, and it lives in your heart. I use my skills to help make a difference in the lives of others through the Make-A-Wish Foundation. I decided to do this because when they granted Irving a wish several years ago, my son was very happy while He endured the chemotherapy process. So, I want to help many children getting their wish comes true. My son Irving was granted his wish for us to go on a cruise together to the Mediterranean—Spain, England, and France. It was a wonderful time together, a beautiful experience.

I am the liaison between the Make-A-Wish coordinator and the families, a role I have been grateful to hold for years. This means that I interview the families to find out what the child's wishes are. I am very sensitive to those families who have non-verbal children because Benny was a non-verbal boy, and I understand how those situations work.

SHARING WHAT I'VE LEARNED

I feel insecure sometimes. I'm afraid of things, just like anyone else, but you know what? I believe that if you have the desire, it doesn't matter how much you struggle or how many challenges you face. You've just got to get on top of it or go around, but you make it happen.

Just make sure that you set goals. What do you want to do? Go for it. We all have different personalities. Some people are more passive, and some of them are more active. No matter where you fall within that spectrum, at the end of the day, if you really wish to have something, you've got to work for it. Nothing is free in life.

Another word that is important to me when I think about setting goals is persistence. I know that when you want something or need to accomplish something, you must be persistent. I have always had goals, but I had to work toward a lot of small goals to get to the big ones. Do one small thing, then another, and eventually, you reach the big goals.

As you work toward your goals, remember what it means to be a leader. I believe a leader is someone who's willing to help others, lift them up, and even become better than I am. Everybody has their own personality, their own goals, and their own situation, but if you are a leader, you want them to be great. When I see people succeeding, I'm happy.

At the end of the day, I believe we are what we achieve, and being resilient has allowed me to achieve a great deal.

BIOGRAPHY

Araceli Zanabria graduated from San Nicholas of Hidalgo University in Michoacan, Mexico and received a bachelor's degree in Agricultural engineering. Araceli is a full-time bilingual REALTOR specialized in Residential sales in the Bronx, Long Island and Lower Westchester since 2002. When working with sellers and buyers she found her true passion in the Real Estate industry providing prime service to the community. Araceli strongly believes in providing honest business, trustworthiness, integrity to Sellers and Buyers during the sale/purchase transactions. Araceli is an entrepreneur living in the State of New York for more than 3 decades. she has owned different type of businesses creating employment opportunities in the area. Aside from being a Realtor Araceli is also a Real Estate Investor.

Araceli is a member of the National Association of Hispanic Real Estate Professionals®. (NAHREP), She is part of the Board of Directors in the Bronx Chapter, she has served as Treasurer from 2019 -2021 and currently She is the President of the Chapter. Araceli is a co-author of a book Today's Inspire Latina Volume VIII; she firmly believes her mission is to tell her story about Benny Jr her son who was afflicted with cerebral palsy and her younger son Irving, who survived cancer when was a teenager. The goal is to inspire other woman with children with any type of disability or kids who battle with any illness that jeopardizes their life

On her spare time, she enjoys spending quality time with family and giving back to society by volunteering her time for a Nonprofit Organization named Make a Wish Foundation, where she works with families whose children are chronically ill. She facilitates the communication between families and the staff of MAW Foundation. She loves seeing the big smiles on each child when their wish comes true!

Araceli Zanabria
LinkedIn: Araceli Zanabria
IG: @araceli_realtor

LEAD WITH VULNERABILITY

———

Erica Priscilla Sandoval, LCSW

"We all have a purpose, and before we move into our higher self, we have to do our own work."

Some days, it's still hard to wrap my head around the stability that now defines my life. For so long, precarity colored everything.

Uncertainty was all I knew as my mother and I migrated from our native Ecuador to Miami and eventually New York.

Fear of what would happen next ripped through my childhood when family members we thought we could trust called la migra on us, forcing us to hide and then flee apartments.

My mother, traumatized, couldn't help but lash out at me for making noise, not cleaning, or being clumsy. All that I could do to protect myself was run to my abuelita and wear two pairs of pants on the days she came home angry, resentful, and exhausted by the daily injustice she faced as an immigrant.

And though my father eventually came to the States to repair his relationship with my mother, their marriage remained tumultuous as they navigated migration, assimilation, and systemic racism.

I thought I would find stability when I went off to college in Florida, but there I failed every class and was the survivor of an unreported sexual assault. I went back to New York, but by then, my parents had returned to Ecuador, and I learned that one of my little sisters was also a survivor of sexual abuse. I was angry, broken, and felt like a failure.

Sensing that I was struggling, my parents told me to come back to Ecuador, that they would take care of everything I needed. But I needed to keep moving forward. I was determined to keep building my new life and break the cycle of intergenerational trauma that constantly left me hanging in the balance.

I tried college again. There, I began to learn about how our behaviors and triggers stem from deep-rooted, unprocessed feelings. But before I could finish my degree, I had to drop out – I couldn't afford the train fare to get to school.

So I threw myself into the music industry and worked my way up to Motown Records' public relations department. Around that time, I had already met the man who became my husband and was pregnant.

I knew where my next paycheck would come from, and I had a home filled with love – finally it seemed like everything was falling into place. Yet I was still struggling emotionally. I was working in a charged environment, and though I was surrounded by people of color, I didn't feel like I belonged. I was in love, but something was missing. I didn't feel seen, and I didn't feel heard. I felt lost.

I couldn't have articulated it then, but I now realize that the roots of my trauma – and the burden I carried from my family's trauma – had wrapped themselves around my every bone and were getting increasingly tighter. I didn't know how, but I needed a way to set myself free.

Freedom came on August 27, 2000, the day my daughter was born. As tiny as she was, Isabella gave me a new perspective on life. I wanted to give her more than I ever had, so I went back to school, waiting tables so that I could finally finish my degree. Although my marriage fell apart and I became a single mom when Isabella was a year old, I had more fire in me than ever before. I worked hard at being a good mother. I joined support groups for single parents in school, began seeing a therapist, and focused on my healing. I wanted to be kind and loving, not cause harm or trauma. I wanted to break that cycle of violence and precarity. I wanted to follow in our matriarch's footsteps and build with love, as my abuelita did.

I tried to give Isabella stability and continuous love, and she taught me vulnerability. She is kind, loving, empathic, and sees the beauty in every rose and every person. She would wipe my tears away when I cried from the exhaustion of working long hours and not being able to spend time with her. I worked Easter,

Mother's Day, Christmas Eve, and New Year's Eve. During the summer, she lived in Ecuador with my parents, while I worked six days a week as a waitress in the Hamptons. She was always so loving when we reunited and forgiving of my absence. I learned how to say I'm sorry and mirrored accountability.

Isabella didn't know it, but she was modeling the vulnerability I had shut myself off from in order to focus on just surviving the first half of my life. My resilience was a security blanket.

VULNERABILITY BRINGS OPPORTUNITY

Fast forward 20 years, and once again, I had the rug ripped out from under me. At first, it was triggering to lose my job during the pandemic, but thanks to years of healing work, I recognized the agency I had to shape my narrative moving forward. I saw this as a chance to strike out on my own and build a business with purpose.

It would have two arms. The first would be talk therapy. It was a gift to work with individuals, especially other Latinx/e, to help them navigate mental health challenges and build their most authentic life. I would fill the niche of supporting the healing of future matriarchs. But I also wanted to effect systemic change, specifically at the intersection of equity and mental health in the workplace, education, and healthcare. We would get employer buy-in by framing investing in their community as crucial to advancing their mission. We are in the people business, and we want our clients to look at ways they can shift their culture to create safe and inclusive spaces.

I believe that organizations thrive when diverse experiences are valued, respected, and included. I wanted to help organizations establish environments where members feel so seen and safe that they are inspired to drive advancement from the inside out. The "new normal" is a working environment that prioritizes honest communication, the mental and emotional well-being of its members, and organizational wellness. With the silent resignation at an all-time high, employees can weigh their options, meaning organizations must shift too. My business helps transform workplaces and educational spaces by enabling an environment that provides the emotional safety for teams to confidently communicate their needs for productivity, nurtures trust and growth, and celebrates diversity. We would show clients that the result is a place that attracts and retains top talent with loyalty beyond a standardized pay scale or the prestige of a degree. People love creating an impact with good people, especially if they feel like they belong.

I planned to target all industries with these training sessions, but I knew social work had to be at the top of my list. Despite it being a profession about bridging gaps in social circumstances and improving mental health, I saw how desperately social work needed to break down systemic barriers and center wellness. And it had to start at the foundation.

Schools of social work operate from a Eurocentric lens that dismisses the specificity of Latinx/e learners. Many Latinx/e social work students struggle to maneuver nuanced dynamics that exist for people of color, like cultural identity, language, colorism, culture, self-worth, and access to resources. Historically, social work programs have taken for granted the willingness of their Latinx/e students to share from their own lives as a means of instruction and failed to recognize the distinct journey that these students have. When left unchecked, these programs reinforce an experience for Latinx/e students that lacks the emotional safety and support needed to be conveyed as a model for future practice.

I experienced it firsthand and knew countless Latinx/e colleagues who had similarly alienating experiences. Because of systemic barriers and microaggressions, only 14% of social workers nationwide are Latinx/e despite that 19% of the United States population is Latinx/e, with even fewer of us holding executive positions in social work.

This new business would strive to have social work schools understand how first- and second-generation-born students have overcome extensive obstacles to get to where they are and have more to face to get to where they're going. We would help schools support their Latinx/e students and staff navigate the cultural, structural, and emotional barriers that arise today so that they're best prepared for tomorrow. I want to contribute to building a social work future where the experts and leaders are from the communities we serve.

I was confident I had the expertise to develop and lead these trainings because of my own discriminatory and dehumanizing professional experiences. As a woman who is a bilingual, bicultural social worker, I had a larger caseload than the average social worker at every organization I worked at.

However, I wasn't paid equitably for these in-demand skills. I've worked jobs where the executive suite was unattainable, and I was never promoted because supervisors told me that I was too good at my job; they couldn't afford to promote me to a new role because they didn't want to have me give up everything that I was already doing so well. Twice, I returned to work immediately after having ACL surgery because I was scared that taking time off to recover would cost me a promotion, a salary line, or even my job. I spent decades moving so fast that I stopped taking care of the innermost parts of myself, terrified that something would be snatched from me if I stopped. I barely took time off and burnt the candle at both ends. Why? Because I always felt I needed to overcompensate for being a Latina.

That's not an accident. Latinx/e are taught that we can't afford to be vulnerable, especially not in the workplace. We come from a place of you just have to keep going, there's no time for rest, hustle to provide for yourself and your family, *pa'lante*. For centuries, whiteness and capitalism have kept our people teetering on the brink of collapse. I've seen how quickly the semblance of security can come tumbling down. Without institutional power or generational wealth, we can't take anything for granted. Though I am seen as a *guerrera*, this *guerrera* became exhausted, and it was not serving me to keep acting as such.

Those are the narrative and cycles I wanted to change. I wanted employers – corporations, small businesses, nonprofits, schools – to see the benefit of treating employees not like "worker bees" but instead like humans whose diversity of experiences, wellness, and psychological safety in the workplace are invaluable to creating a better product or service.

For this reason, I named the business Sandoval CoLab. The name honored the expertise I was bringing but also stressed the collaborative nature of the work we'd be doing to build stronger environments and connections.

I knew that to lead authentically, I would need to center equity and wellness within my own organization. That was how I would build a team that was excited to work *with* me, as opposed to for me. Our workplace would be kind, compassionate, humanizing, and validating. I had felt the toll of previous workplaces where colleagues, especially supervisors, invalidated my work or refused to acknowledge it. These microinvalidations made me feel invisible and taken for granted, nagging feelings I still fight. I committed to celebrating my team, even on the little victories. I want them to know how much I value the time and unique talents they spend on our work.

Being so honest with your team is vulnerable, but I knew that the best leadership stemmed from vulnerability. I had been raised to think of leaders as erratic, closed-off geniuses who pride themselves on being invincible. But I was set on embracing my entire humanity in order to accomplish my mission and lead my team.

Not coincidentally, my leadership turning point was also my most vulnerable. Shortly after launching Sandoval CoLab, everything started to go blurry. I would walk into my office and not know where to start. Everything seemed urgent but impossible.

Building the plane while flying it left me overwhelmed, anxious, and depressed. I went to see a neuropsychologist about what I was feeling, leaving with a diagnosis of ADHD, attention deficit hyperactivity disorder. Finally being able to put a framework to what I had been feeling empowered me to share my struggle with my team. I opened up about what I had been facing and how I needed them to support me. Instead of hiding the "mess" from them, I let my team in.

That vulnerability kickstarted our success. From there, we hired more clinicians and expanded Sandoval CoLab's clientele. We booked more wellness and equity workshops with New York University, Brown Brothers Harriman, Comunilife, Cushman & Wakefield, Sony Music, Prospanica NY, the New York City Department of Social Services, Trinity Church of Wall Street, Mount Sinai, Microsoft, Palo Alto Networks, Boston Children's Hospital, the United Federation of Teachers, and the New York Psychotherapy and Counseling Center. We also published four books in English and Spanish in collaboration with 44 leaders in social work. All in less than one year. Instead of allowing this diagnosis to cripple me, I decided to make it my superpower. I continued my own healing journey and discovered ketamine-assisted therapy, a true game changer.

I then became a ketamine-assisted psychotherapist to guide clients in immersing and connecting with their soul through psychedelic journeys. I now host retreats nationwide focusing on integrating your psychedelic journeys into your daily life with an open heart. I realized the connection to self-made me a better

TODAY'S INSPIRED LEADER VOLUME IV

leader. I was kinder, more forgiving, accepting of mistakes, less critical, and projected less of my own insecurities onto others.

That same year, I was invited to become the New York Socia of Latina Empire, a testament to my passion for supporting intergenerational trauma healing. My vulnerability allows me to provide tangible tools to the communities that need it most while increasing access to mental health and holistic wellness techniques.

As my business thrives, I'm watching my team glow and begin to lead with purpose too. These women are owning their power. This makes my heart swell. A leader doesn't hoard the talent and future of their team. A true leader makes space for their team to succeed on their own terms and facilitates opportunities for them to soar beyond the confines of your vision and organization. I'm proud of the future leaders I'm helping produce, regardless of if they help me grow my business for the next decade or if they leave a year from now to chart their own path. I just hope they also lead with vulnerability.

I've never been one to seek out leadership; it's a heavy burden. As the eldest child in an immigrant family, and the oldest of sixteen grandchildren, I was the one who translated for my family and navigated spaces on their behalf. I didn't ask to take on these responsibilities, but I had to nonetheless. My parents and sisters looked to me to lead. In my career, I've always focused on just doing the work. I bring people together, advocate, organize, build, and then hand it over to the next leader who I am mentoring. But once colleagues and people I shared space with started to look at me as a leader, I had to acknowledge the power I held and the change I was creating. I didn't crown myself a leader. My community unwantedly bestowed that title on me, and it is a heavy responsibility. We have to acknowledge the power we hold and constantly recognize the privilege we have in order to not cause harm and instead help others thrive and believe in themselves. Because a true leader is never alone. We pass the baton to others and make sure everyone wins. We are all leaders. We just need to believe in ourselves.

I wouldn't have become the leader I am today without the many mentors I've had. The foundation of seeing other people believe in my dreams and ability came from a high school social worker who took me under her wing. For years, I held onto what she told me: "You can do anything you set your mind to." Collaborating with social work *madrinas* Dr. Linda Lausell Bryant and Dr. Richeleen Dashield has helped me heal old wounds and given me an opportunity to lead with heart and purpose. Dr. Jacqueline B. Mondros has helped me see myself as a change agent, an organizer, and a system disruptor; she has helped me envision the long-term goal of my work. As I've developed my businesses, Fig Factor Media Founder Jackie Camacho-Ruiz has been integral to helping me navigate marketing and storytelling. I've also been incredibly fortunate to be mentored by Perla Tamez Casanovas of Latina Empire. My story demonstrates how mentorship can take many forms and nurture different parts of your leadership journey.

Now that I'm someone who has some wisdom, resources, and connections, I'm focusing on being a mentor myself. I want to share the lessons I've learned and empower the next generation of social workers, entrepreneurs, and equity leaders who've had the cards stacked against them. I don't want to help fill social work classrooms, executive suites, and board rooms with Latinx/e, immigrants, and people raised in poverty simply for the sake of it. No, this is part of breaking the cycle of harm that relegates us to spending our lives searching for healing. Instead of focusing on the past, we'll be able to focus on the present, our future, and our children's future.

As an inspiring thought leader, I provide tools, resources and knowledge to empower the next generation of matriarchs who are the center of family systems by motivating them to break the cycles of intergenerational trauma and helping them manifest their goals, all while owning their narratives. Building connections with people helps me strengthen communities, and that is when collective healing begins.

I believe in the power of narratives and our ability to change the world through our stories. I believe in one community, united through the fabric of inspiration. I believe in the AMAZING power of mentorship. I believe in the undeniable potential of the mind. I believe that we can thrive with the right tools and knowledge. And I am ready to share them with the rest of the world. I hope to activate 1,000,000 matriarchs, no matter at what stage in their lives, to own their narrative in the United States and beyond.

We all have a purpose, and before we move into our higher self, we have to do our own work.

DON'T BE AFRAID TO FAIL

Leading with vulnerability means not only becoming comfortable with failure but also being public about it. Failure in itself is neutral; it's just an outcome. But our culture has attached negative meaning to failure, and we live in fear of it. We've become so afraid of it that the idea of failing can stop us from trying something altogether. That is such a loss because failure is rich in lessons about how to move forward.

But it's also critical to note that failure doesn't happen in a vacuum. At times, I've failed because of the legacies of colonialism, racism, poverty, and other systems of oppression. Like 40% of Latinx/e and 51% of Black social work school graduates, I failed my licensing exam. While I eventually passed, I'm now part of the movement that is advocating to reimagine and implement different systems in lieu of an exam that has kept generations of social workers of color from earning a higher salary and obtaining more equitable positions. We're letting the failures of the past fuel us toward a more just future.

I am so open about the times I've fallen short or something hasn't gone my way in order to destigmatize failure itself and shine a light on its systemic underpinnings. May we learn from our failures and be propelled by them.

TURN ON YOUR SOUL

When you wake in the morning, you may open your eyes and think of all the things you have to do. You may think negative thoughts, such as the weather sucks or you hate your job and having to go to work. You may recognize a pain in your body or remember a worry you had the night before.

Let's try something different. Don't reach for your phone and scroll. Don't turn on the TV and watch the news. Turn on your soul instead. Keep your eyes closed and take five slow deep breaths. In through your nose, hold for five seconds, and out through your mouth. Put your right hand on your chest, and feel your heartbeat. Imagine a pure light entering your heart and it opening up slowly to allow that light in. Say these words to yourself as you feel that bright light enter your open heart, "Today is good. As I share my talents and gifts with the world, today is good."

The world needs you. You are also a leader, and you have a purpose.

BIOGRAPHY

An immigrant with a heart of gold and a zest for life arrived in the United States with big dreams. Little did she know that she was going to face some of the hardest moments of life in her quest for success. She wanted to make an impact, but did not know how. Little by little, mentors appeared to guide her on this new journey. She realized that she had the power to change the narrative of her life. She realized that she did not have to be the immigrant victim, the single mother. She realized that she had the power to change her reality. Through education, mentorship and volunteerism, she found herself in a beautiful ecosystem she created, and every day the sun was shining brighter. Every day, her dreams began to manifest right before her eyes, and she believed more and more in the power of her dreams. Now as conqueror, *guerrera* with a trajectory of impact, she is ready to help 1,000,000 matriarchs do the same. She is Erica Priscilla Sandoval, LCSW.

As a mental health practitioner, speaker, executive coach, entrepreneur, podcaster, philanthropist, and author of *Latinx/e in*

Social Work Volumes I and II. She founded Sandoval Psychotherapy Consultation – known as Sandoval CoLab – where she oversees a team of social workers; leads diversity, equity, and inclusion work; and provides ketamine-assisted psychotherapy, a breakthrough approach to an awakened mind and healing trauma and depression. Erica was recently named New York Socia of Latina Empire, a personal and business development coaching program.

The recipient of many awards, Erica received Prospanica-NY's 2021 Top Latinx Leaders Social Justice Award, was recognized by Latino Leaders in Action as a Latino Leader on the Radar, and was awarded the Make-A-Wish Foundation's 2018 Diversity and Inclusion Innovation Award. In 2020, Erica became the first immigrant Latina president of the National Association of Social Workers' New York City chapter and is now the chapter's President Emeritus. She served on the board of directors of Latino Social Work Coalition Scholarship Fund Inc and mentored the new leaders of the organization.

As a proud immigrant from Ecuador, her passion is fueled by supporting the community she is a part of and their children. Her greatest pride is being a single mother and raising her 22-year-old daughter, Isabella, whom she considers her biggest teacher.

Erica Priscilla Sandoval, LCSW
Latinxinsocialwork.com
IG: @latinxinsocialwork
Sandovalcolab.com
IG: @sandovalcolab
LinkedIn: Erica Priscilla Sandoval, LCSW

LEADING THROUGH TRANSFORMATION

—

Karina Mejia

"Love not only who you are but what you are capable of doing."

I was born a warrior, but there were moments throughout my life where I didn't believe I was. Born in a small neighborhood called Callao 6 miles away from Lima, Peru, I was part of a dysfunctional family, dealing with the abuse of my father and having to live in a shack with him and my mother in the Angamos neighborhood just outside of Lima. I admit that things were not the way that I wanted them to be, spending most of my childhood in situations that no child should have to go through. For years, my parents fought and our home became a place of domestic violence. This wasn't the life my mother wanted for us, but at the moment, there were no other options.

When I was 16 years old, my parents went through divorce and soon after, my mother made a bold decision to move to

Mexico. We moved to a country that had an entirely different culture than what we were accustomed to in Peru, not to forget emotional toll that the divorce had on the family as we no longer had to live with my father—it was devastating to see my family broken apart.

So, with fear emitting through our bodies, we relocated to a world with a distinct culture and set of rules when I was sixteen. After witnessing familiar things go and having to adapt to so many novel circumstances, these encounters made me feel unique, which helped me connect with immigrant families now because I once experienced what they are currently having to. My experience with moving to Mexico was tough in several ways apart from the difference in culture and custom. Moving to a new country meant starting over from the very beginning, and leaving what we once were behind, but I trusted my mother.

My mother has always been my biggest influence, even to this day. She has been the strength that I have to keep pushing forward because despite all of the unfortunate circumstances that she has gone through, her motivation to keep providing for us and creating an environment where I could thrive and feel safe never failed.

Wherever we moved, I knew that she did it with the intention to give us the best life that we could have after leaving our once dysfunctional family. My mother didn't graduate high school, but that didn't stop her from making sure that I didn't follow the same path she once went down because she knew the strength I had hidden within and wanted me to unleash that to the best of my ability. So, without an ounce of doubt in my body, I followed every idea, advice, and guidance she gave me, which made me the leader that I am today, promising to her that I would one day give her the great life that she truly deserved. To this day, she continues to give me the guidance that I need to better serve my clients and those around me.

I believe that in addition to her, my rough childhood is the reason why I decided that I wanted to help others that are struggling to find the right path in life. I vowed to myself that I would help others that are suffering with themselves or in abusive relationships to find that peace within themselves to turn their lives around. I didn't want anyone to experience the trauma that I had and if they did, that I would help them move on from it in a healthy way. But I knew that getting there involved a long road ahead, the first step being a path to healing own past and understanding that what I experienced is something that ultimately shaped me to the person that I am today.

Once I took the time to analyze my past, I realized that I wanted to become someone that helps individuals find the strength to improve their lives and that so I decided to become a therapist and inspire and serve families and help them transform their lives for the better.

FROM PSYCHOLOGY TO LEADERSHIP

It was a teacher at my university that discovered that my talent for helping others can be used as a teaching method. She told me that there was a school that was looking to hire a teacher with my type of qualifications and that I should apply, to which I did and was hired. From there, I soared new horizons as I was not only given the opportunity to teach students, but to learn as well. Here I was able to obtain a master's degree in family and couple's psychotherapy, thus completing my education and beginning my career in psychology but as much as I wanted to help others, it wasn't that easy because not one individual is the same.

Having the opportunity to serve others through therapy has its obstacles, one being that you have to understand the person in order to teach them how to understand and love themselves. Throughout my career, there were many times where it was easy for my clients to open up, but with others it took time because they need to know that they can trust you, especially after the trauma that they have endured.

One of the most important tips for building trust is to love the person you are intending to help wholeheartedly, meaning that you have to understand who they are, including their strengths and weaknesses, and still love them while showing them that they should love themselves as well. Part of the journey to success is to teach them to love not only who they are, but what they are capable of doing because then and only then will they begin to heal and learn to help others.

BUILDING A COMPANY FROM ITS FOUNDATION

There were many moments where I felt that I could not continue with the career I have always loved, but it wasn't because I didn't want to help people. I knew in my heart that I was born to help others, however there were situations that I felt that the methods that I was choosing to help others weren't benefiting them, which took an emotional and professional toll on me.

One of my biggest regrets was that I so driven to helping others, that I burnt myself out in the process because I believed that being a leader meant giving the people you serve everything but being left with nothing in return. I did not realize that I was emotionally and financially draining myself while helping others fulfill their goals and begin their own path to healing. I lived like this for a long time before I realized that I was wrong. From there I realized that if we want to dedicate our lives to helping others, we must find a balance between taking care of them and taking care of ourselves.

When I decided to open my own company, Infam Instituto Latinoamericano, I experienced a lot of downfalls. In addition to this, my company has experienced many hardships including not being able to pay the rent, services, or our employees. With creating an entire company from scratch, there are risks that have to be taken and things that will not always go your way, but that doesn't mean that they will stay that way. I had thought that I had failed with my company, but that was when I realized that I was far from it.

In order for me to continue to help others, I knew that I had to learn to organize my own life to have the ability to serve to the best of my ability. One of the rules I strongly live by is the 80/20 rule. With this, if giving your 100% is impossible, giving just 80% will be enough for you to achieve the goals you set for yourself. Every morning, I stand in front of the mirror and remind myself that I don't have to be perfect to achieve the goals that I set for myself and that whatever I accomplish that day, even if it's small, is a step in the right direction. We must learn to celebrate all of our accomplishments, even the small ones because by celebrating our small steps, we reach a level of happiness because we were able to accomplish a task necessary to get to that bigger goal.

The one mistake you can make when building something from the ground up is to quit when things go south because if we were to quit every time we encountered a challenge, we wouldn't have had half as many accomplishments as we would if we kept going. Its normal to fail at times; it's human. We must experience obstacles, especially in the beginning, in order to be prepared for bigger obstacles we may face when our company is thriving.

THE MEANING OF LEADERSHIP

To many, leadership is defined as leading someone to success but to me, it means much more than that. Leadership doesn't always have to do with professional success, because if you focus making the person succeed without knowing them, you have failed as a leader. I personally define it as a method of transforming others to a better version of themselves. With every person you impact, you leave a mark in their life as you were the person that helped them see a version of themselves that they hadn't realized before. If your leadership is done right, you leave that person with a better understanding of themselves and that their past doesn't define what they can become but instead can be used as a tool to keep pushing themselves to lead them down a path of success professionally as well as personally.

You have to focus and gravitate towards transformation because in order to have success, you have to have inspiration and legacy to get to where you want to be. Two of the most important characteristics to have in order to be a leader is having the natural ability inspire and show others how to transform themselves because without inspiring others to want to become better versions of themselves, they won't be able to reach the potential that they hold within if they aren't able to unlock it.

Throughout the years, I have learned that difficult situations are necessary for one to transform themselves. By placing yourself in an uncomfortable situation, you allow your mind and body to forcibly step out of your comfort zone and deal with the situation regardless if you're uncomfortable. I have taught myself to constantly put myself in this position by setting goals for myself that I know will force me to step out of my comfort zone. I do this because those moments where I have felt very uncomfortable are doing me a favor. They are teaching me that not everything will be handed to us and that we must encounter the moments that we find uncomfortable and uneasy in order for us to understand how to overcome them and keep moving towards our goal.

THE PANDEMIC

As we all know, the pandemic was a traumatic experience for all of us, physically, mentally, and emotionally. From losing loved ones to being trapped in isolation for several months, we suffered moments where our mental health was heavily affected. As a therapist, this period in time was the most crucial for my company because clients came to us more than ever wanting to improve the damage to their mental health and needed our assistance to help them make that first step. This wasn't easy for us to do as we had to experience the same environment that our patients did.

Nevertheless, we opened our doors and offered our services to anyone that needed them, ready to unlock the trauma trapped within their souls and begin their healing and transformation process. During the pandemic, we had the pleasure to help transform 17,000+ professionals within the mental health industry in Latin America, which I still cannot believe. What began as a period of despair and trauma quickly unraveled into moments of opportunity and healing. We knew that the only way to help others was to reach them through mental health was through education, which is why we sought out to help mentor those professionals and teach them the "intervention and effective therapy model", where they are able to find a change in their patients in just the first session.

Although, we had to digitalize our services during the pandemic, that didn't stop us from making the impact that we were able to make to not only our clients, but other professionals across Latin America. The professionals that we have transformed have in return helped us impact 68,000+ families/individuals and begin the process of healing from within and creating their own path to success, making us not only the proud recipients of the 2022 "Sueña en Grande" award, but brings us one step closer into free ourselves from the trauma we hold and becoming more than we believed we would.

WHAT DO YOU NEED TO BEGIN YOUR JOURNEY TO LEADERSHIP?

1. Make sure that God is present in your life and have faith in Him. Ultimately, He is the one that makes all the decisions and without Him, nothing would be possible.
2. Find within yourself and your strengths something you are passionate about to the point where you can talk for hours about it and not get tired of it and make sure you have clarity.
3. Have short-term and long-term goals and objectives to be able to unleash your passion and move towards your dream.

ACTIVATE YOUR FIRST STEP INTO LEADERSHIP

I encourage you find a space where you feel the most peace. Find time during the day to sit there and be grateful for what you have. Look around at the things and the people you are surrounded with and be grateful that you have them as part of your life. There are moments where we focus on what we want and forget about the things that we already have. Next, visualize what you want to accomplish today and set goals for yourself. What steps do you need to take in order to get to the place you want to be? What do you need in order to accomplish your goals?

BIOGRAPHY

Karina Isabel Mejía Gastelo is a Family and Couple Therapist. She is the creator of the methodology "Terapia Efectiva", mentor of psychologists, therapists and psychiatrists. As specialist in Brief Systemic Therapy, she has more than 16 years in the professional practice of psychotherapy.

Karina accompanies people to activate their resources, to be happier and more productive, emphasizing on the processes of change and processes of change and solutions to problems. She is truly committed to the exciting challenge of being brief and effective in the intervention she performs with her clients, with the firm commitment to bring out the best in the best of themselves.

Throughout her career, Karina has worked with hundreds of families generating greater awareness of the importance of prioritizing mental health in the Latino community.

community. She is the founder and director of INFAM Latin American Family Institute, Clinical Case Manager and Director of *Emociones Magazine.*

Karina is actively sharing her message in 17 countries, creating courses and certifications for women, couples and families. and certifications for women, couples and families with children and adolescents. She is an international lecturer, creator of the 21 days for a conscious and committed relationship program and presenter of the podcast "Terapia Efectiva".

Karina Mejia
hola@metodoterapiaefectiva.com
IG: @karinamejiaterapeuta

LEADERSHIP THROUGH PERSISTENCE

Leonor Gil

"God does not call the qualified. He qualifies the called."

The above quote has a profound connection to my journey of leadership. I have oftentimes not felt worthy to be called a leader and this quote reminds that God chooses the individuals that have a pure heart of service; something that I have always felt in my heart.

The word and meaning of "leadership" bring back so many memories from various stages of my life. Perhaps at the at that time, I did not attribute it to this, but as I grew older, I felt a deep connection to showing up as a leader. You see, my childhood and upbringing were not an easy one and I even struggled in my adult years with embracing my self-esteem, oftentimes being shy and quiet.

Now in hindsight, looking back, I certainly can identify the times that answered the call of leadership in various situations, always connecting back to my core, making swift decisions to help others.

EARLY EXPERIENCES WITH LEADERSHIP

I still remember the day that my mother had to embark on a long journey to the United States of America leaving my brothers, sisters, and I behind with our grandparents. I remember her disappearing in the distance as I wiped the tears off my eyes. Although I was only five years of age, I have that memory in my mind as if it was yesterday. I knew that I would not see her in a long time and that I had to be strong for my siblings and show up to help my grandparents in this new role as parents. There were many moments of sadness and despair as I thought about my dear mother and what her days would be like. I missed her every single day and I tried to stay occupied to make the days go by faster. How can I single mother of four sacrifice herself so much for a brighter future for her children? I just knew that one day I would make her proud for her hard work.

For some reason, I was constantly put in situations of leadership as a young girl. It was as if God, was vetting me for the years ahead.

At only eight years old, I remember how we used to travel to Guadalajara or Morelia with my grandparents and I would be the one answering questions about the water or electric bill and other adult matters. I had to figure out a way to help them, they were counting on me.

The years that proceeded would be marked with constant opportunities to show my leadership skills. Now in the United States at the age of eleven years old, reunited with my mother and family, I would be asked to organize my family's hectic schedule and manage the payment of the bills, attending important appointments and translating. That mindset of taking the lead on a project was also present in my days in high school, I took the initiative to get involved with sports, and the Math, Science and Latino Clubs. My desire to get involved and show up for others was always there. I needed to belong, but most importantly, I needed to contribute.

You see, when no one in your family is pursuing such involvement and you have no role models for what it looks like to be successful in that way, the best place to look is inside of you. What do you want to achieve? What is it that you truly feel inside your heart that you want to achieve?

A moment that marked my life forever was one day that I was riding the bus. For some reason, I was realizing the difficult situation that my family was in, with my mother working two to three jobs, endless days, and constantly trying to get ahead. We were still undocumented at that time and therefore, we did not have many options. It was a sublime moment when I made a promise to myself. I promised myself that I would do my best to be successful to provide for my family. I promised that I would work hard to change the direction of my family. I promised to take advantage of the opportunity this country was giving us. I never forgot that promise. To this date, it is engraved in my heart.

My opportunity to identify my true calling was on the horizon when I got the opportunity to start my college journey at the University of Houston. To my surprise, this "melting pot" of cultures and backgrounds gave me a broader view of the world and embrace multiple cultures as I solidified who I was and continued my pursuit of success. I, again, became involved in clubs and organizations that would allow me to expand my knowledge and learn about others. This new ecosystem of relationships that I created would help me face difficulties while in college. For once, I realized that the education at a university was much more difficult than high school. Even though, I was a top student in high school, I was really struggling with my classes. My major was accounting, and I was flunking it. For a moment, it would bring my memories of that shy and low self-esteem girl that I was growing up, but since I had made the promise to myself to do my best, I made a decision that would change my life forever; to change majors. With the help of my uncle, who became one of my biggest mentors, I changed my focus to finance. Little did I know that that decision would bring about the success that I envisioned while helping build other leaders and make a difference in the community.

ACCEPTING LEADERSHIP

Soon after I graduated college, I landed an amazing job

where I was the only woman and Latina in the role. It was not easy. I did not have experience and experienced a lot of criticism.

By the time, I was married to a very controlling and abusive person, eight months pregnant and working on my securities license; one of the most difficult to obtain in the financial world. I worked tirelessly to get my license, spending three hours three nights per week at the library after long days of work with a baby in tow. This six-hour test was one of my biggest challenges at that time. I was exhausted but had a mission to accomplish. Afterall, I had made that promised to myself.

Not only was I able to get the securities license, but I secured two more difficult ones. The persistence in my heart was a true testament of my ongoing commitment to success. I wanted to make my family proud. I wanted to pave the way for others to let them know that they can achieve success too.

I was soon found in a position of leadership, in a position of impacting others. Through becoming a Senior Vice President at a global financial firm with over thirty individuals under my supervision, I knew that I would directly impact their lives. Every time that the review period would come up, I would take my time to review each one of the employees, their journey, their capabilities, and potential to make sure that I really got to know them. I would oftentimes sacrifice time with my own family to make sure that I was prepared, and I was the best leader to them that I could be. I was one of only 2% of the leaders in that position and I took that very seriously.

After dedicating over twenty years of my life to this global financial company, I found myself in a very difficult situation again. Due to an unexplained business decision, I was let go of my position. This situation became another important adversity in my life. This incident greatly affected my self-esteem, evoking emotions of sadness and lack of self-worth. I knew that in those two decades, I had given my best. I had always shown up as a great leader and elevated others. My reviews told that story. My salary proved that. My accolades supported that. Even though, I was dumbfounded by that decision, I could not continue asking myself questions that I did not have the answer to. I had to remind myself of every single moment when I chose to continue, when I chose to take another step in the direction of my dreams.

I had to do an inventory of all my accomplishments and separate myself from the business decision so that I can gain the clarity and objectivity for my next move. I knew that I had to move fast. I could not be stagnant. I could not stand still, but most importantly, I could not blame myself for that decision. To my surprise, and as gift from God, I reconnected with an old mentor just two weeks later. She reminded me of my worth, my abilities and potential. She reminded me that there was something bigger and greater for me to fulfill my vision to help others. Doors started opening. Previous relationships re-activated. Knowledge resurfaced. I had to draw upon my confidence, my experience to allow me to decide fast. Trusting my gut and intuition supported by my desire to share what I knew with others, I aligned with several leaders to start my own business.

SHARING LEADERSHIP PRINCIPLES WITH OTHERS

Fast forward to today, my commitment to serve others through my example continues to be alive and well. Now, as an entrepreneur, I get to directly impact individuals and families to achieve financial abundance. With my over thirty years of experience in the finance world inspired my uncle, backed by my successful journey earning six figures for a long time, and having proven my commitment to elevate others, I bring that vast knowledge to truly help others.

My journey has been paved by struggles, doubts and oftentimes fear, but there has always been this feeling of there being something greater than me guiding my steps. A force of nature that allows me to see bigger than myself, centered in giving and serving others. The idea of paving the way for others inspires me to never give up.

THREE KEY INGREDIENTS TO LEADERSHIP

Persistence, resilience and believing in yourself are three important ingredients to becoming that others recognize and get inspired by. Persistence allows you to keep moving forward, to never ever give up and stop the pursuit of your dreams and goals. Resilience reminds that you that you are born to achieve those goals despite the adversities; it is an inner feeling of achievement that allows you to look ahead. Believing in yourself even you have not arrived yet, gives you direction and purpose. All these ingredients are paramount in your journey as a leader. As I navigated and learned many lessons, I remind myself constantly of my purpose through these ingredients. How can you apply them to your life today as you show up as a leader in your community?

HOW CAN YOU BEGIN YOUR LEADERSHIP JOURNEY TODAY?

1. Focus on your goals - every day (the last couple of years, I hold a vision board party with our family, took a risk and everyone was in!)
2. Education
3. Set your priorities- manage your time wisely to make it happen with discipline
4. Learning constantly - sharpening your saw

HOW CAN YOU SPEND YOUR TIME TO ALIGN WITH YOUR PURPOSE?

Personal development- Never stop learning. Take time to read books, listen to audio books, podcasts and interviews. Learn, learn, learn.

Professional development- Attend conferences, workshops, seminars within your industry and outside of it to give you objectivity. Constantly think of what is new and fresh in your industry and how you can get ahead.

"Me" Time- Take time for you. Take time to decompress, to think, to strategize and to connect the dots for your health and mindset. You deserve the best and if you are well, you will be able to take care of others.

My legacy: to know that I did at least a little something to change the way that I do things.

I hope that with my story and leadership journey, I can pave the way to help you recognize your innate leader. After all, *God does not call the qualified. He qualifies the called."*

You are born to be one.

BIOGRAPHY

Leonor Gil is a professional in the financial services industry with over 30 years of experience acquired as Senior Vice President at a top global institution, and as Director of Operations for Harris Associates L. P., a prominent Chicago advisory firm. Leonor is passionate about creating and implementing strategies to promote an inclusive and diverse work environment. Areas of expertise include process improvements and management, personnel management. Over the years Leonor leveraged her strong business acumen by developing a panoramic view of the business working across various disciplines including Finance, Technology, HR, Compliance, Client servicing to name a few.

Leonor is an advocate and strong supporter for diversity and inclusion and has served as the Treasurer, Secretary, and Co-Chair of the Professional Development Committee of the Latino Council. Leonor received the Chairman's Award – D&I in 2017 and the Mujeres de HACE Leadership Award in 2018. Leonor has been featured in various publications including

Profiles in Diversity Journal Magazine, Revista Agenda Mujer, and the Daily Herald's Business Ledger, Influential Women in Business. Leonor enjoys sharing her knowledge participating in different panels including, Finance, Diversity in the workplace, and Mentoring Circles.

Leonor enjoys positively impacting the lives of others by volunteering for Big Brothers, Big Sister for United Way and as a Confirmation Facilitator at her church. She serves as a mentor to co-workers, and to young Latinas for The Fig Factor Foundation, where she has served as a board member, Secretary, and Treasurer. Leonor is a published contributing author in Today's Inspired Latina Volume V.; the soon to be published Business Divas; Stories of Women Leading in Business and Today's Inspired Leader Vol. IV.

Leonor's motto is to "Live to Serve, and Serve to Live".

Leonor received a B.A. degree in Finance from the University of Houston, is fluent in Spanish, holds several FINRA licenses including Series 7, 24, 63, is a Life License producer, and has a Mentor Coach Certification.

Leonor is a proud mother or two children, Jorge and Carol, and a proud grandmother to four grandchildren; Destiny, Anthony, Santino and Jaylani! Leonor loves to travel! Her hobbies include hiking, dancing, and spending quality time with the family.

Leonor Gil
LinkedIn: Leonor B. Gil
IG: @leogil12

THE POWER OF NUMBERS

———

Martha Razo

"In the language of numbers, there are infinite possibilities and infinite horizons. And with numbers, we are limitless."

Coming to the United States from Mexico and growing up in Chicago with my family, my driving force started very young. As a top student attending Chicago's Curie High School, it was always my dream to attend college, but others had different opinions for my future. I wanted to apply to college and I was told no by various people. They said I should settle for working as a cashier or an employee in a grocery store because I was an immigrant. I was an undocumented immigrant at that time, but now I have my residency. People told me I wasn't going to go very far or even go to college because I didn't have a social security number. That really angered and frustrated me. I used that energy to locate resources at nonprofit organizations, and those contacts told me about scholarships opportunities. I was 15 years old at the time.

I was confident about finding ways to apply to colleges, but at the same time I was torn in the sense of what I wanted to do for my career. When I applied to colleges I wanted to be in theater because my passion was acting and speaking on stages. When I appeared on stage to give presentations, people called me the future Oprah Winfrey. I got all excited and transformed even on the inside. I felt very special. On different occasions, people chose me to be a spokesperson. I believe that is my gift—talking to people to motivate them and bring them light and energy.

Seeing where my enthusiasm and heart was, I applied to the best theater school in New York and I was admitted. I had no training in theater or speaking; I learned from doing. At that time, the school accepted only 10 students from the Chicago area.

I was super happy and on cloud nine. What concerned me, however, was how expensive the tuition was so I looked into the school's scholarship opportunities. When I said I was an undocumented student, the representative abruptly stopped the conversation. With an angry and incredulous tone, she asked "What are you even doing in our schools?" and "What are you doing in our country?" It was so mean for someone to talk down to another person in that manner. She literally crushed my spirit, and my happiness and motivation fell by the wayside. It was at that moment, I stopped going to school and doing my homework.

If I ever showed up to class, I wasn't present. Internally, I wanted to die; I didn't want to live another moment. I dug myself deep into a hole, mentally and academically, and I didn't see a future for me.

One moment, though, kickstarted my will to live. The turning point was when my high school counselor told me I wasn't going to graduate because I needed an extra English class. I was a very high-achieving student, and now I was going to throw everything away. No way was I going to let this happen. I needed to graduate, at the very least. That is when I picked up the slack and asked every teacher what I needed to do to pass their classes. By doing that, I graduated in 2012 and attended Illinois Institute of Technology (IIT).

ALWAYS GIVING THE BEST

While attending college, I saw a glimpse into my future through the workings of my parents Chicago-based company called Guero's Pallets, Inc. The company provides wood pallet solutions including custom-built pallets. The company was the starting point for me to build my own business: SOLiX Business Services, and to reignite my interest in math. Working at Guero's, I started to see how mathematics, finances and data processing played important and often decisive roles in helping businesses stay afloat in good and bad economic times.

My Dad gave me the opportunity to work for him in 2014 after we "broke up." What I mean is that I left his house with my boyfriend when I was 18 years old, and that broke my parents' hearts. I was tired of living under a kind of strict Mexican rule.

When I was growing up, you saw the unfairness between girls and boys. For example, the guys can go out, and the parents don't question them. But the girls had to be home and be really good. So, I left my home at 18. My Dad did not talk to me for a year and that broke my heart. To pay for my college tuition, I worked for Chipotle. I had to pay about $6,000 every semester. Working for Chipotle was not the best experience. One time, I made guacamole, and then I accidently dropped a large amount of salt. My co-workers were not very happy, but they fixed that batch. The staff moved and kicked me out of so many different stations.

For instance, they kicked me out of frying chips because I burned myself. I got kicked out of peeling onions because I was crying and very slow at doing it. They had a timer and I had to peel them at a certain time. I also tried my hand at cleaning the fountain drink area and the bathrooms, and I was terrible at doing those things, too. Despite my difficulties, I always asked what else I could do? I always had a positive mindset even though I wasn't the best at these jobs. I think that that's why they kept me. They always wanted me to be there. Even though I will burn my hands or make a salty guacamole, I had this attitude of "Let's get the day rocking. I'm burning your place up, but let's do it."

My Dad always said to me "no matter what you do, don't just do it to do it. I mean give it your all." Whether I washed dishes, burned my hand or hand fried those chips, I was trying my best, but was probably not the best compared to someone else. Even making guacamole, it wasn't the best, but for me it was. I always give my best.

ADDING UP THE NUMBERS

Eventually, I left Chipotle, but I also needed financial help to continue my education. That's when I asked my Dad for help. He gave me a company job and chance though I thought he had an attitude of looking at me as just a hired worker. Remember, he was still mad at me for leaving home. Some roles included cutting wood with a table handsaw, driving a forklift and operating a much larger machine that cuts thicker wood pieces. I used that same mentality of a positive mindset and observation on how to move a forklift and cut boards. Knowing that I was getting a Master's degree in applied mathematics—I earned a Bachelor's of Science degree in applied mathematics and math education from IIT— I wanted to do something better than working in a warehouse at my family's company. Watching those guys work there was amazing. I was kicking their butts when it came to cutting boards. It took me three months to do that.

Growing tired of these tasks, I asked my Dad if there was anything else I could do. He gave me the office work position. I visited his office and it was a very old trailer with a shoebox filled with papers. He was old school in everything he did. He was a one-man show doing everything from being a forklift driver to moving trailers to handling clients' phone calls to managing accounts receivable.

My job was to review and manage the financial books. I was scared because I didn't have a background in business. I only knew how to organize things and a math background. That didn't stop me from finding other resources that could assist me. So, I started learning about QuickBooks. Before I did that, I looked at his bank account. I told him that he was overdrawn by $3,000 and to stop making checks. That was the moment he said to me: "Well, that's why I have you here." It dawned on me that this job had some serious responsibilities. He gave me the reins to manage his accounts and to save his business.

I learned everything I could to ensure the finances were all in one place. I collected from businesses who owed us money, learned about our vendors and clients, insurance policies and contracts, negotiated the best prices for lumber, and kept track of our trailers in Illinois, Wisconsin, and Indiana. In our line of work, we drop trailers at our clients' location and they stay there. When we deliver the pallets, we switch out those trailers. They can get lost if we don't track them and people want to steal them for metal. So, I developed a database for tracking these trailers.

We were renting and wanted to own a facility. I used what I learned from my math degree to prove to somebody that we qualify for a loan. It took us two years to convince the bank to lend us money for our own place and in 2016, we finally bought our facility. This year, we paid off the loan and the 2.75 acre property is ours. To our family, that's a big deal.

I looked at our revenue numbers, and we were always at $4 to $5 million. Our profit margins sucked where we would be between 3 to 5 %. We were only making money to pay expenses and supporting everyone else. Then COVID-19 happened. Many people thought that we got lucky because during this time prices for materials doubled. Now, as I analyzed the situation, many companies took the wrong strategy. I heard a lot of companies went out of business during the pandemic, even some of our competitors.

To prevent us from experiencing the same fate, I used data analysis to develop forecasting models. The marketing, production and finance information went into a monthly report. Those reports showed my parents how they can gradually make small changes every month. With this method, along with a strong team and a strategy in place, we grew our business from $5 million to $10.1 million in 2021. Our profit margin went from 5% to 35%--a seven-year increase! Knock on wood, this year I hope to get us to $15 million. That's my next target and I'm going to write it down so that it happens. When you write things down and believe in them, they happen. Eventually, I want our company to get to $100 million in sales.

KNOWING THE NUMBERS

In order for business owners to be successful, they have to know their numbers. There are no shortcuts. Business owners have to know their numbers and I'm going to preach to them to the end of my life. Tell me how many people have built million dollar companies? There are very few people who have done this, and I'm one owner who has built a business. Read "Rich Dad, Poor Dad." Talk to Donald Trump and all these rich people. They will tell you that to be successful, the core message is to understand your numbers. To be successful, in general, you have to have goals and direction. So, know what your objectives are and think ahead of the curve.

Let's say you have a vision board, and you think about a number in mind for a certain goal. It's usually about numbers, sorry to say. A number is a metric. For example, I want to purchase a three acre property. You put that number out there, write it down and then start taking small steps to achieve that goal. Every day you have to ask yourself if this is going to get me to that three acre property. If it's not, then just change course.

SETTING HIGH GOALS

I would say dare to dream big. When you expand your mind and say "Okay, I'm passionate about this project or I want to be at this level," don't be afraid of setting that high goal. I say that I want to get to $100 million in sales. It sounds ridiculous. Someone is probably laughing at me when I say that but it's OK. It's OK if people laugh at you if you dare to set a high bar because this is what happened. Even if you don't get to $100 million, $25 million or $50 million, I would have never imagined that if I did not dare to dream big.

I have my own vision board. Before, I would journal my thoughts about what I wanted to accomplish. For this year, I've accomplished some. I helped my parents invest in properties while I managed them. I'm also raising money for my nonprofit called The 2% Fund. My mission for this organization is to increase the number of undocumented students enrolled in higher education through financing and mentorship. For this, I wanted to raise $10,000, but we received a grant for $11,000, and we also raised some of the funds. Altogether, we have $15,000. I know that it doesn't sound like a lot of money. I didn't even think it was possible, though, because we were getting $4,000 here and $5,000 there. So, $15,000 is three times more than what we were usually doing for my nonprofit. Other things that I'm working on is getting 50 national accounts for our pallet company. We have about 15 accounts.

As of 2021, we're neither a national account nor a national supplier in 2021. But, in 2022, I said we have to supply nationally. We have 17 states that we're supplying pallets to outside of Illinois. I'm also doing my bachata dance classes every Friday and trying to wake up early every day. I was forced to do that because my son started kindergarten. Lastly, I want my husband, son and my family to be together and happy.

TAKING THE FIRST STEP

I tell people when they are thinking about their own missions and goals to just start. They are spending and wasting time thinking about when they are going to do something. They should start and do it. And, it's OK to fail. All of us fail. I'm failing at many things too, but that's OK. I'm learning from my mistakes and that's why I'm capable of doing so much. It's really the rate at what you learn from your mistakes that will determine how successful you are.

And just because you failed at something, you shouldn't quit on it again. You will quit if you don't get any enjoyment or fulfillment. However, if it does give you enjoyment and fulfillment, it makes you stronger and more knowledgeable in what you should and shouldn't do.

I do what I have to do to stay positive. If I think that something's not going to happen, or I'm not going to pass this test, or people aren't going to like me, then I'm bringing negative energy to myself. I have to always be optimistic and moving. I hang on to my joy and optimism because that is my fuel. With God on my side, I will be unshakable and unbreakable.

In addition to my optimism, I also know I'm capable of anything. If somebody tells me that I now have to run the military, what do I do? Well, I don't know anything about the military or about weaponry. But I'm sure that I'm capable of learning anything. I want to tell everyone that they are capable of anything and learning anything. But the real questions to ask are: "Is it worth it?" and "Is it what you love?" You should never stop yourself from doing something because you think you can't do it. No, anyone is capable of doing anything. You're even capable of learning my math. But is it worth it? Is it worth your time? Is it your interest? If it's not your interest, why would you spend all those hours?

SHOWING BY EXAMPLE

Leadership, for me, is like guiding someone by the hand at first. That person is watching you since you are the role model. When I feel that someone is ready to do the task or project without any help, I make sure I'm at every step with that person and then also ask him or her about the confidence level. I think that's what you have to be a leader. You have to be vulnerable to be wrong and to be questioned by others.

In the process of all this, you're also learning. I think the second that a leader thinks he or she knows it all, it's a mistake. Now, if you are training an individual or a leading group of people, you need to show vulnerability because by doing that, everyone can work together in strengthening and supporting each other. Say if someone is strong at doing something specific and the other person doesn't have that knowledge, they probably complement each other. So, when you see each other's weaknesses, then you can compensate for each other's strengths.

BIOGRAPHY

Martha Razo is a business consultant, mathematician, engineer, philanthropist, entrepreneur, writer, and CEO of Guero's Pallets and co-founder of SOLiX Business Services. Martha has a Bachelor's and a Master's from the Illinois Institute of Technology in Applied Mathematics and is pursuing her Ph.D. in Industrial Engineering at the University of Illinois at Chicago with a focus on data and process mining. Martha is also the founder of the 2% Fund, a nonprofit whose mission is to increase higher education through financing and mentorship for undocumented students. Martha is your business and numbers expert. She has used her Master's degree in Applied Mathematics, along with 10 years of business experience, to build a national, multi-million dollar company. Her experience as a business owner and consultant ranges from restaurants to properties to manufacturing and spans clients throughout the nation. If you are feeling stuck in your business pursuits, uncertain about particular decisions, or looking to expand your business Martha's services will benefit you. Martha's knowledge and experience will help grow your business.

Martha Razo

www.martharazo.com

LinkedIn: Martha Razo

CHANGING THE WORLD WITH INNOVATION

—

Olga Camargo

"Don't walk in anybody's shoes, make your own shoes."

I have a firm belief that my purpose on earth is to help make it a better place. I do believe that there are things that need to be fixed, things that need to be improved, and opportunities that need to be opened. I believe that I am here to make a difference. I have been on a journey that has really illuminated for me what it is that I need to do at this point.

I was raised in Chicago's Little Village Mexican community where my family owned a successful business, so I always had the impression that I was wealthy. When I was in college, I began reading books and became aware, through those experiences, that I lived in an underserved community. I had no idea that my family lived in a poorer area and that our financial situation wasn't great.

Within a Latino household, the topic of financial matters was never broached. It was an unwritten code of conduct. It never occurred to me as a kid that the food I was eating might not have been good for my body or contained essential nutrients; we just ate whatever my parents bought. When I look back on it now, I can see that my parents were financially unable to purchase foods that were better for us. I realize that if people were paid more, or at least the same as everyone else, it would open a lot more doors in terms of accessing higher quality food, education, more housing options, and amassing wealth to also leave something for our loved ones.

It was a wake-up call for me when I was in college, and I started reading about people who were similar to me. It was then that I realized that despite having grown up in the context of a family business, we should have been in a better financial position.

My mother owned a bridal shop, and I helped my her out. I was not even an employee. I was just helping her out all the time because that was expected. I learned a lot from her on how to run a business, how to handle customers, and how to make sure to meet deadlines. She was an intelligent woman, great at math, and had many other talents, but she only spoke Spanish. I remember one specific moment when I was about fourteen years old when a financial representative entered her shop's door and tried to sell her some financial product. I remember the guy was trying to communicate with my mother; he only knew English, and my mother only knew Spanish.

So, they looked at 14-year-old me, hoping that I could translate the business between them. The guy looked at my mom and spoke, then they looked at me, I translated, then they both look at each other again, then I translate, and the next thing you know, he's no longer looking at my mom. I didn't realize until, in hindsight, how he had basically dismissed her. She had vanished at that point, and suddenly, he was talking to a 14-year-old to help him seal his deal.

The transaction did not happen because I couldn't really understand or translate the financial product. It was confusing. I see my early personal experience lived out today repeatedly by so many within our community. There is a real problem in how our community is addressed by the financial industry and it needs to change. There must be a genuine investment to learn more about how to genuinely approach our community and ensure that our community's financial needs are being met. Unfortunately, some representatives are just trying to find the easiest way to make the sale.

In many instances, there is confusion amongst the buyers as they may not be sure of what they just purchased and have unanswered questions that include: Was it the right fit for them and their business? Were the fees reasonable? What options did they have? They hope at the end it will all work out. This was an eye-opening experience for me growing up, learning about this persistent problem, and seeing firsthand the inequality that was taking place due to lack of understandable information.

Once I earned my bachelor's degree in business, I went to work for the financial industry; however, I remembered that whole incident back at my mom's bridal shop and knowing that our family like many others don't speak finances at the kitchen table. In my mind, my community's financial guidance and education needs have always been front and center. I realize that finances are complex and difficult to understand by many people in the U.S., irrespective of language even though language barriers exacerbate the issue. So, we need to reflect on how to best address that lack of information in our community so that everyone can make informed financial decisions.

I thought to myself what things were causing issues for my community. So, within the financial industry, I went into investment advisory, specifically wanting to help non-profits with their organization's retirement plan and help get their employees retirement ready. Rather than only focusing on assisting one person at a time, I decided to raise the bar for myself and help one organization at a time. Before starting my work with the organization, I researched its existing 401k investment lineup, I quickly learned that it was not optimized to benefit the plan participants and their beneficiaries. I knew then I needed to sometimes start from scratch and completely overhaul some these retirement plans to give employees a better chance to grow their portfolios. Of course, that also included ongoing monitoring of investments, actively working with the organizations' leadership and providing financial education to plan participants in English and Spanish. All of this allowed me to learn and gain more insight on the many issues that our minority communities were facing as they tried to plan for retirement.

I decided to work at a larger scale immediately when I became an investment advisor to the C-suite. The CEO of an investment management firm was a mentor of mine and always told me to think big and that the sky was the limit. He told me repeatedly that I could do whatever I wanted. I had enormous respect for him because he had come from very humble beginnings, and yet here he was, the CEO and chairman of an investment company. I believed every word he told me because he was living proof that it was possible. He was self-made and worked his way up the corporate ladder and made a difference. He passed away but I always remember him, and I try to make my own difference in this world.

I thought to myself, having been mentored by somebody of that stature believing in me. The more he believed in me, the more I believed in myself. When you see someone that has gone through tribulations picking themselves up when things get tough, it ignites something inside of you. To be able to walk into a room and hold a specific vision, a particular type of thinking that no one else has, and they come to you, and want to hear what you're thinking, it confirmed to me that I was on the right path.

GIVING A VOICE TO THOSE HIT HARDEST

After the pandemic hit, a record number of Latina women were let go from their jobs or left to take care of their children and families. Now, as they are trying to come back to work, we are still dealing with the widest pay gap in the United States. I knew one again that I needed to elevate my professional work to address the economic issues that Latina women are facing.

Working with other Latino leaders, we have designed and are building a Latina fintech app not only for the Latina community but also for anyone else who can relate to the challenges that Latinas face as they try to build wealth. We want them to acquire financial knowledge and ways in which one can amass wealth. Our mission is to spread awareness about the importance of securing themselves financially and their families. There are a variety of ways in which we can assist them with this application. We offer education on money management so that they can increase their wealth and assets. They need to put their attention and understanding on retirement savings and how those things function.

In addition to this, we provide access to financial resources, such as financial advisors who genuinely care about the community and want to assist in the education of those who live in underserved areas. We want to provide them with tools for wealth planning, and for Latinas who own their own businesses, we want to assist them in gaining an understanding of their net worth and working within a budget.

The capacity for strategic career planning and advancement

equally stands out as the other app feature. There is guidance on how to negotiate salary or ask for a promotion at their place of employment. There is a phase of career planning in which they are assisted in mapping out where they want to be and how to be proactive with managers and supervisors to get promoted.

We are trying to work within the confines of the system that is in place, but we are also aware that you must be proactive. It is not enough to sit around and waiting to be acknowledged. There is a need to take the initiative and ask, "This is the destination I want to reach; what is the best way to get there?"

Therefore, when I consider other fintech apps in a broader context, I realize that those other fintech apps do not understand Latinas. They are, for all intents and purposes, ignoring their genuine needs. In addition, we have found that some of the other fintech apps currently available are not suited for Latinas or other minority groups. In general, Latinas have the impression that mainstream fintechs are not talking to them when they discuss topics such as yachts, and vacations in Europe, and fail to embrace the family in their offerings. Latinas wish to acquire the skills necessary for success, but they are not receiving those.

FIGURE IT OUT

When there is something that you want to do, you need to take the time to figure out how you are going to do it. Don't rush the process. Too many people just head straight to the point and never think about how they are getting there or why they want to get there. You need to sit down and think about it. Study your feelings and emotions. Maybe the problem is bothering you or making you question where you are. You need to reflect and find out why you feel those things instead of just jumping off the train. Sometimes it's our own fear that gets in the way of us succeeding. By anchoring ourselves to the problem and really taking the time to figure out a solution, we can better ourselves and our thought processes.

You might start walking in the direction of that possible solution, but then it gets a little bit vague, and you don't know what happens after you go in that direction. Then think about who around you, you can talk about this issue with. I have learned in life that figuring out tough items on your own is too hard. Don't do that to yourself. We're all human. Work with other people. And you know what? They will help you with your ideas. Either they validate them, they help enhance them, or they help you find the solution.

And then, when you have the solution or things that need to change, then you need to execute. You need to believe in what you need to, in what you know needs to be changed. You need to believe in that, and you need to act. It's not enough for you to have ideas. It's great to have ideas but significant ideas you need to take action on. You need to execute. Take a little chunk of whatever you think you can do, and stop and think about what is wrong, what needs to happen, and execute. You got to believe in yourself. If you know what's wrong at your core, chances are that's, that's what's going on.

FIND YOUR SPACE

Everyone wants to offer you support. You should not have the impression that you are going through this by yourself. And if you feel the need to discuss the issue but are unable to zero in on the specific cause, then you should talk to other people. They are able to provide the insights that you possibly do not have, which you require assistance with. And that, my friend, is the point of this life. Figuring out what's going wrong is the first step. There are a great many things in this world that could use some sort of improvement. And since we can all benefit from it, why don't we all pitch in to make it even better?

Someone who is a strong leader will have the ability to recognize when another person is having difficulty with something and will want to assist them. The feeling of accomplishment that comes from being able to mold what you're working on to where it needs to go or change things to where it needs to be is very satisfying. It appears you are really making progress toward your goals. That you are the person responsible for that change and that you are a leader. Right now, we could use some more strong leaders. Also, you need to think about the field in which you want to be a leader.

The fact that people regard you as someone who, number one, cares about what is happening and, number two, rely on you to make change because they already recognize you in that space is rewarding. Also, maybe I'll be able to collaborate in other spaces where there's some intersectionality and work with other leaders and grow intellectually. Because the world is not the same world that we lived in, not even five years ago, there is evolving leadership and innovation. This is because the world is constantly changing.

BE HONEST WITH YOURSELF

Being conscious of who you are is, in my opinion, is the most essential step that you can take. Consider your identity. Realize that everyone, regardless of where they are in life, possess both strengths and weaknesses and that there is always an opportunity for you to improve yourself on a personal and professional level.

Put yourself in the company of those who always have an optimistic outlook on life. It's possible that some of them will wind up becoming mentors and will have uplifting and encouraging things to say. Have the humility to recognize that you do not know everything and to seek clarification when necessary. You can pick up a lot of helpful information from talking to other people. It makes no difference whether they are more or less experienced than you are. You can always pick up something new from other people. And I'm here to tell you that you can make that dream of yours a reality, no matter what it is. You need to be able to act freely to pursue those dreams; consequently, when you notice that a door has been unlocked, revealing a path toward those dreams, you should not hesitate to enter through it. Don't even bother to entertain the thought. Because there is a possibility that the door may close, go through it immediately.

FAILURE WILL HAPPEN

I have learned the most from some of my mistakes, and as a result, I will never make those mistakes again. Therefore, you should always look on the bright side and be okay with accepting defeat. Many people are unsuccessful. Everyone that you see out there, including a significant number of leaders, have been unsuccessful at something. Nobody is without flaws. That individual does not exist anywhere on this planet. Because of this, every single person will always have something that they are not very good at or something that they are not as powerful at, even if they do not consider it to be a failure. It's possible that they'll simply say, "I'm not as strong here, but there's always an opportunity to enhance it." The same thing applies when you make a mistake; now, you have an opportunity to improve. Because gaining wisdom through mistakes and experience is the best way for us to improve ourselves.

BIOGRAPHY

Olga Camargo, AIF® has over 20 years of experience in the financial services industry. She is the CEO and Founder of SHENIX™, a fintech app built for Latinas and helps close the wealth gap to accelerate their economic and social transformation through culturally compatible financial education, professionally qualified Latino/x advisors and career coaches that speak English and Spanish. Olga is also a Partner at Toroso Investments and provides investment advisory services to individuals, businesses, and nonprofits. She specializes in servicing the Latinx community. Olga is the National Board Chair for the Hispanic Alliance for Career Enhancement, served as Forbes Business Council's Financial Services Chair (2020-21); and is a 2019 Aspen Ideas Festival Ricardo Salinas Scholar. Crain's named her among "Chicago's Most Powerful Latinos". She serves on the Illinois State Treasurer's Hispanic Advisory Council, and Illinois Latino Legislative Caucus Foundation's Economic Development Committee. Olga earned both her Bachelor of Science in Business and Master of Arts in

Language, Literacy and Rhetoric degrees from the University of Illinois at Chicago. She holds the Accredited Investment Fiduciary or AIF® designation, an ethical certification issued by Fi360, formerly known as Center for Fiduciary Studies, and the Uniform Investment Adviser Law Examination, Series 65 License.

Olga Camargo, AIF®

LinkedIn: Olga Camargo, AIF®

INVEST IN PEOPLE AND MOMENTS, NOT THINGS

Priscilla Guasso

"The most powerful moment as a leader is when you realize all the keys to doors you have and you become purposeful in how you give them away."

During my childhood I had a desire to do something great. What was that? I had NO IDEA. All I knew was that God had given me a basket of very different talents that I'd use someday. I started to play a game in my head after every goal I accomplished, where I would find myself asking the question, "Was this the big thing I was meant to do?"

As the years progressed, I pridefully poured myself into my

amazing career as a human resources leader and thought, "Was this my big moment? Is this the big thing I was born to do?" While I continued to have a flourishing HR career in hospitality, healthcare, and technology, I had a moment in my life where I questioned heavily the very topic of this book and how this would connect to the larger legacy of my life.

What kind of leader do I want to be, and was my life modeling that in every aspect of what I do?

LIFE, HEALTH, AND JOB CHALLENGES

A few months after I pondered these very questions, I realized that I was missing something in my career. So, I made a giant leap and joined another company that brought my husband and I back home to Chicago where I elevated my career as a human resources (HR) executive.

As proud as I was to have reached an executive level in HR (my dream!) I found myself constantly stressed and not enjoying a big part of the role there: managing a revolving door of employee relations cases and diving into the least favorite side of HR for me - investigations. Don't get me wrong, for some of my closest friends they love this part of HR...but for me each day was soul-crushing because this is not where I get energy. As great and organized as I was in working each case thoroughly, I was crushed that the role wasn't the dream I had thought of in my mind. I wanted to lift careers, develop leadership capabilities and impact our future in DEI. As this was happening, God has a funny way of grabbing your attention and mine was through my health. I was reminded during this time that we only have one life and what we do with it isn't by chance. We make choices at every opportunity - good or bad - to move towards a dream or against it.

After being honest with myself, talking to my husband, and deciding to put my health first, that's when I decided it was time to leave. I wasn't full of zest, excitement, and energy. Life is short, and I didn't intend to waste any more time.

It was also at that time, in early March 2020, that I went on a mission trip to El Salvador and like many others have discovered on trips like these, you think you're there to change the world for others, but it's your own world that changes.

When I got home, I reaffirmed to my husband that I needed to leave my job to root back into what was my foundation, and he said, "Ok. Let's figure this out." We left our beautiful apartment that I referred to often as the ivory tower overlooking Lake Michigan and Navy Pier, and we moved into my sister's basement to save money and still cannot fathom how we shared one bathroom amongst six people.

This was one of the hardest moments—concrete floors, fun spiders that would surprise you at night, and no big windows to let you know if it was sunrise or sunset. As much as we all tried to make it feel like a "home" I'd be lying if I didn't share that there were days I would ask myself through tears if I had made the right decision. I was an HR executive that should not be living like this. As hard as it was, this decision created space for us to have flexibility to face the unknown and we made unforgettable memories with my sister and family during the pandemic that I will forever hold in my heart. Just ask me for the pictures, they tell the best stories.

The whole reason I left my role was to build back up my personal foundation and that was exactly what happened. I was reminded that a title and salary should never define you. As I continued to believe this my world began to change and the realization of who I thought I was going to be as a leader reignited a new direction and purpose.

THE NEXT BEST MISSION

After much introspection, I realized my next mission was to build and create Latinas Rising Up in HR. It became my own space, my dream, and my vision. Many encouraged me, including Jacqueline Camacho-Ruiz, who simply said, "Let's make it happen."

Two books and a new venture later, we have built a community that I am extremely proud to lead. Following my passion in connecting Latina HR leaders across the globe has brought on a new sense of purpose and vision. To have the honor and privilege to be a part of the growing stories of each of our authors and members shows me that ONE person can make an impact. We just have to trust and act.

As I reflect on the title of Today's Inspired Leader, to me that means in the limited time we have here on Earth, I want to keep creating waves—those ripple effects that impact the hearts and minds of those that I have the honor of working with, whether that be in my career as an HR professional or in my business as a coach and speaker.

I know that I am also a leader who is honored to have the opportunity to give fruitful advice and help others in ways that I didn't have before, all because I fell into HR and have grown an amazing career from passion, service, and gratitude. While I've always been a leader; I now know what I want my legacy to be and trust me, nothing can stop you when you believe in yourself and have purpose.

COMING FULL CIRCLE

Where I am today has taken me full circle, back to what I learned from my mom about connecting with others, listening to their stories, and seeing their heart. And my dad, too, who encouraged me to never stop learning and to search for guidance, resources, and remember the fruits of being resourceful.

I am able to see now, as I look back, how I had to travel that path, to learn, to experience the good, the bad, and everything in between. I can see how beautifully it all worked together to bring me to where I am today.

Without any one piece of it, I wouldn't be the person I am today, with the knowledge, skills, resources, and determination to build something that helps others every day. If I had any doubts about that, there are plenty of women who have taken the time to tell me the impact Latinas Rising Up in HR has had on them, and words cannot express how grateful I am.

When I was young, I felt this calling to do something big,

and I know I'm not alone in that. I really believe each of us has something inside that drives us, that big thing that calls to us, but I don't think there is an end date for it. I believe there is always something bigger and better and more amazing that you can do in this lifetime. Becoming the leader you are meant to be is only the beginning of your journey.

You won't see results overnight because it takes hard work, pain, honesty and time. It may sound crazy but fight hard to find joy in these moments of pain. You will learn and grow from them. Then, move on to the next thing, the next step, the next goal.

Take the time to let life occur around you. That is when those life-defining moments happen.

WHAT HELPS ME STAY CLOSE TO MY MISSION

In order to stay close to my personal purpose, I try to make time to pray and meditate. Being a person filled with energy this is extremely hard, but I find so much clarity when I can stop and just dream. I also try to find ways each week to inspire a few people who come to mind that I think might need something–words of encouragement or compliments when I see they're doing something amazing online. Or I might feel a tug at my heart to send them something, and I act on it when I think about it.

It could be something as simple as a handwritten note to say I'm thinking of them and I hope they are having a great week, or I might ask if there is something I can help them with. I can't send 20 a week, but over time, the number of people you can touch adds up...even doing it once a day would mean you've acted on lifting up 365 souls in a year.

I know how much it has meant to me when someone has taken a moment to fill me with inspiration at a time when I needed it most. It's something I love to do after I've already focused on filling my cup.

INSPIRATION IS MY GOAL

As we each grow into our own leadership styles, know that leadership means something different in every job and for every person. In my 16+ years, I've seen leaders who were downright cruel and others who are uplifting and inspiring. I personally believe servant leadership is the key and clearly shows who are the true leaders. It's seeing who they are and what they do behind closed doors, through their actions, how they listen, follow through, and encourage innovation.

As I grow and learn from amazing leaders around me, I am more convinced that *the most powerful moment as a leader is when you realize all the keys to doors you have and you become purposeful in how you give them away.*

After years in my profession, going through my own personal growing pains and taking action to never stop learning, I challenge myself and those around me to focus on spreading copies of our keys of change and inspiration. If I can support any person around me to get to the next level in their careers and in their life, to connect with others, and inspire them on this life journey, that's what I'm in for. As much as I love my career, at the end of the day my purpose resides around people and their personal journey. We're in a world now where lines and boundaries are extremely blurred. My hope is to help us not forget who we are as individuals and what gives us zest for life to give our best in all we do.

I believe all of us have something in us that drives us. But being in a hustle-minded culture that can easily consume us, I challenge myself often to take a page from the book of life written by the many elders in my life, to stop and smell the flowers so I don't miss the important things around me.

It's about being present in the moment and asking questions as I did when I was a kid. It's also being curious outside of the socially acceptable question, "What do you do?" I want to know what lights you up and motivates you. What are you known for? How is your family and what are your dreams?

As I lead initiatives around leadership with different teams across different organizations, the number one issue I hear about is on trust, psychological safety, and relationships. These three areas are the foundation—the pulse—of every team.

As I continue to grow in my personal journey, I care little about what your title is and more about the legacy you want to leave behind. I want to know more about how you're bringing others up through your influence, power, and resources. Life should be more about the journey, which can be hard in a results-driven society.

This is my personal struggle bus, but I work on it knowing I'll never have all the answers. As I am figuring it out, I have some of the most amazing people around me that feel invested in, cared for, and valued. I continue to be supported by friends, family, mentors, and sponsors that speak encouragement into me to be that leadership catalyst who is creating a change.

I encourage you to lean into your curiosities on what brings you joy, freedom, and purpose. Take account each year of who you want to spend time with and why. What value does it bring and how do you reciprocate?

At a certain point in your life, you're going to have this similar moment where you'll look back and think, "What do I want to spend my time doing and why didn't I think about this sooner?" Give yourself grace and know that you've been gifted with so many keys of knowledge and success…it's up to you to decide what you're going to do with them now.

BIOGRAPHY

Priscilla Guasso is dedicated to unlocking the keys to connections and communities.

She is a talented, energetic, and driven woman who instinctively sees the potential of others, connects them to their mission by embracing their curiosities to help reveal the purposeful leader they have inside.

A skilled human resources leader, Priscilla has focused on all areas of the employee life cycle: talent acquisition, mobility, talent development, succession planning, performance management, employee relations, global diversity, equity and inclusion, and overall company culture.

With global HR experience since 2006 in the US, Latin America, the Caribbean, the UK, and Canada, Priscilla has spent a great deal of time in the hospitality and healthcare industries. Today, she's a leader in the talent management, development, and diversity team within the technology industry.

Through her business, Manifesting Leadership Group,

LLC, Priscilla coaches and trains leaders in corporate, startups, nonprofit, and government agencies, giving them opportunities to invest in themselves to effectively grow their leadership skills.

As an Amazon best-selling author and founder of Latinas Rising Up In HR™, she continues to give back by creating a community of Latinas in HR and their allies, sharing their keys to knowledge and success, and opening doors to unlimited possibilities.

Priscilla holds a Bachelor of Science degree in business administration with a concentration in marketing from the University of Illinois, Urbana/Champaign. She is a popular and in-demand speaker known for her vulnerability and touching on topics in personal development, DEI, allyship, combating your inner critic, and embracing failure.

In 2021 she became a contributing author to Volume 9 of Today's Inspired Latina™, was a speaker for the 2021 LATINATalks Global Tour, and has served as a proud board member of the Fig Factor Foundation.

During the 2020 pandemic, Negocios Now recognized Priscilla as a Latino 40 Under 40. She is also an annual inspiration agent for Young Latina Day and a proud member of HRHotseat, Hispanic Star Miami, Society of Human Resources Management (SHRM), and The Latinista. She is also a past board member of the National Hispanic Corporate Council (NHCC), Mujeres de HACE Chicago, and the Latino/Latina Alumni Association for the University of Illinois.

Based in Miami and Chicago, Priscilla enjoys traveling to new cities with her husband, Jorge, spending time with close family, and soaking up the sun in warmer climates.

Priscilla Guasso
www.latinasrisingupinhr.com
LinkedIn: Priscilla Guasso

LEAD WITH CONFIDENCE

Paulina Lopez

"Leadership always starts with you. It comes from within. You cannot lead others if you cannot lead yourself."

The success stories of many Latina leaders start with humble beginnings centered around culture, family, and living a better life in America. What makes the journey different is what led us here, our unique paths, personal story, the decisions we made and where our choices took us.

My story began in the Caribbean, on the island of the Dominican Republic. I can still remember the sense of freedom of being in nature and enjoying the outdoors every single day. We spent most of our time with family, and conversations always centered around food and future plans.

When I was four, we immigrated to the United States. The culture was very different. It felt transformational... in a good way. We settled in a small apartment in Long Island City, Queens. It was a big change in our daily habits and our lifestyle, but somehow it brought the family closer together. It overlooked the beautiful Manhattan skyline, and signified opportunities, possibilities, and change!

My uncle and grandparents were already here, and the goal was for the entire family to make their way here. It was the vision of my uncles to follow the American dream. It changed the family dynamic for the better, as they pooled their resources to build a foundation and establish themselves by purchasing real estate in the US.

Growing up in New York City, I learned a lot about diversity and the different cultures. Just being part of the public school system was very interesting. It was a creative outlet and a very profound experience for me. Being Latino and low-income, we were able to take advantage of the different programs offered which shaped my world.

Looking back, it instilled a confidence in me that later provided lots of opportunities and opened many doors. I see now how my resiliency started at an early age, through my passion for dance and the arts. It led to recognizing the power of projecting authenticity from that uniqueness and creativity.

A CONFIDENCE BUILDER

Those fundamental years played a pivotal role and

developed critical skills. I had teachers who influenced me in my youth. Some played a key role, by taking me under their wing. They saw something in me, and they guided and mentored me. They helped to build my confidence through performance and showed the importance of creating meaningful relationships and deep connections.

Throughout my teen years, I found a sacred space and sisterhood in supportive groups and dance crews. I thrived in building a community. It was another outlet to build my confidence and leadership skills. I noticed the difference in myself, how I had changed and evolved, and I felt there was a level of maturity that kicked in for me early on.

I remember my senior year of high school some friends and I would wear business suits to school. Silly really, but I felt myself already tapping into that entrepreneurial spirit. A mentor once said, "You have to dress the part and faith it 'till you make it." I didn't know what being an entrepreneur looked like back then, but I know that building my confidence and faith shaped my vision.

THE TURNING POINT

In the Latin culture you follow a certain trajectory where you get married, have children, and build a career, so I did all that. I was married in my early twenties, had my daughter shortly thereafter, and I began my career in corporate. Juggling all this, was where I started to lose myself.

I lost my sense of inspiration and motivation to do more

for myself. I was taking care of my daughter, a husband, working many hours, and neglecting myself. I began experiencing burn out. At some point, I recognized it just enough to separate from the relationship, which was emotionally challenging in many ways.

I was able to rediscover what I had lost, picked myself back up, returned to school, and climbed the corporate ladder. But it came with uncomfortable growth. As I was redirecting my life, I experienced the lowest point of my life and the turning point. I went through a horrible divorce and custody battle that was my wakeup call!

In the midst of this, I had a mentor once ask me the one thing that changed my world. "How can you take responsibility for this situation, and how could you have avoided it?" That allowed me to reflect, and the best thing I could do for myself was to explore how I could take responsibility for this. How could I start taking responsibility for everything that happened in my life? I could choose to shift it or change the direction, and that was the key.

From there, I began the serious and deep inner work, hiring coaches, and attending workshops, seminars and wellness retreats. I started to invest in myself, my personal growth and development. And without realizing, it re-sparked many things in my life, specifically the entrepreneurial spirit. That's when everything shifted.

As I began rebuilding my confidence and reflecting, I asked myself "How can I do more? How can I be more?" and "How can

I make it happen now? How can I shift the direction of my life? How can I take full responsibility for how I want the rest of my life to look?"

Entrepreneurship was what gave me that vision of what I've always wanted to do. I started to take charge, and seek resources and opportunities, despite the challenges of being a single mom. I was able to redirect my life, and the changes felt amazing! I was excited about my future.

INVEST IN YOURSELF

My corporate career was in finance and human resources. Both gave me collective skills, strategic guidance, and valuable expertise. The most valuable experience was in human resources where I witnessed firsthand true potential being denied opportunity, based on how they looked on paper. I became an advocate for ambitious, driven individuals, and thrived in identifying and developing leaders.

In finance, I excelled in creating systems and structures to simplify and streamline operations. Growing other businesses motivated and inspired me to pursue my own entrepreneurial path. It was at this time that I started my side hustle, supporting and consulting small businesses part-time. It took a lot of commitment, sacrifice, and boundaries to stay laser focused on my vision and my goals.

I spent my evening and weekend hours doing part time work in finance, bookkeeping, and auditing. I discovered the challenges small businesses had and the lack of resources and information when it came to funding, tax savings, and strategic guidance for growth and sustainability. I was supporting these small businesses as an independent contractor, and it was growing with time.

Meanwhile, in my career I was getting signs that it was time for me to take that leap of faith. So, I did. I launched the consulting firm full-time, but replacing the salary was not happening fast enough. The greatest transformation came when I finally gave myself permission to hire a business coach for my own business. Once I invested at that higher level, I started seeing results!

The journey of self-reflection and deep inner work, along with the professional skills made my entrepreneurship path successful. I used all of my experience and the tools that I had been given to create a strong foundation in my business. I stayed consistent, removed distractions, kept it simple, and continued investing in myself.

BUILDING COMMUNITY

Today, I lead the Business of WE community of Women Entrepreneurs in New York City. A tight knit, trusting, supportive community with a collaborative spirit of success. The Business of WE is about bringing women together in sisterhood and camaraderie as we grow our businesses, because we all learn from each other!

I realized how my journey led me to the work that I do today in leading this community of businesswomen and entrepreneurs. We focus on building the right relationships and strategic alliances. The greatest feedback I get from the community is that it's a sacred space that helps them open up, feel supported, share, learn, be heard, and be held accountable.

Business requires that you build authentic relationships, get out there, network, and explore opportunities. We provide maximum networking opportunities at our highly interactive meetings, conferences, mastermind groups and wellness retreats while featuring other businesswomen, leaders, and industry experts.

The great awakening and power pause of 2020 literally paved the way for more women to bring about their gifts, talents and values into the world in the greatest way possible. During such confusing times, it was humbling to see women step up and show up, by changing the game in business, and we need more of it! The community came together stronger than ever.

TIPS FOR SUCCESS

My journey from corporate, to consulting, to community helped me learn the importance of the personal aspects of every business – the mindset, the inner-work, your environment, your working space, and your community. Having a strong foundation and the right systems and structures is a very effective way to have more clarity, focus and productivity. Because everything starts with you.

A few of the daily habits I've incorporated into my life are two-hour nature walks, journaling, meditation, and a self-care morning and evening routine. Making time for yourself is critical to avoid burnout. I highly recommend you be mindful of the information you're consuming, the news, radio, and television. Especially how you start your morning because it can make or break your day.

Building a business and leading a community is about having a genuine interest in other people, being authentic, compassionate, and understanding others in a more intimate way. That's always been my gift. I'm grateful to have people confide in me. That came from my years in human resources.

I've had strangers say, "I don't know why I'm talking to you about this." I think it's due to the welcoming energy. No judgments, just 'how can I support you?' with no hidden motives or agenda. Just compassion and understanding. Because when there's confidence, clarity, and honesty about you, others are naturally drawn to you.

Interestingly enough, I've had some people dismiss me as maybe irrelevant or someone that they didn't need at the time, and I get that; it is human nature. You can never take that personally. Always have faith in yourself and your abilities. I've had people come back to me and say, "I underestimated you."

On the flip side, it's important to understand that not everyone is in your corner or should be a part of your inner circle. Not everyone is ready for that level of collaboration. When I sense negative or competitive energy, I have a compassionate conversation. Communication is everything. That's the secret to creating a sacred space, protecting your community and leading with confidence.

Remember, leadership always starts with you. It comes from within. You cannot lead others if you can't lead yourself.

BIOGRAPHY

Paulina Lopez is an Author, Speaker, Business Coach, Consultant and Strategist. Her Corporate Background is in Finance, Operations, Strategy, Human Resources and Communications. Paulina is CEO and Founder of The Business of WE (Women Entrepreneurs), a tight-knit, trusting and supportive community based in New York City. The Business of WE brings together minority business women and entrepreneurs, through their highly interactive workshops, mastermind groups, summit conferences and wellness retreats. They are dedicated to providing the necessary resources, essential strategies, innovative resources, support systems, access to capital - and the clarity, motivation and inspiration needed for personal and professional success. The trailblazing women of this collaborative community are taking control of their work life, initiating more startups, generating income, driving innovation, creating wealth, joining forces and leading communities worldwide!

Paulina Lopez
paulinalopezconsulting.com
LinkedIn: Paulina Lopez

FROM MEXICO TO MICHELIN

Yanitzin Sanchez

"I live by one word: love. If you don't add love to what you do, you won't get the result that you expect."

Growing up in Toluca, Mexico, I remember having a very beautiful childhood. I grew up with two brothers and a cousin named Juanito who I considered my best friend. As the only daughter in my family, I was my dad's favorite.

Both my paternal and maternal sides of my family had wonderful cooks. My maternal aunt who recently died—I called her Mi Tita—had a real talent cooking dishes, especially important meals. For instance, in Mexican tradition, if someone was celebrating a birthday, you had the traditional dish of mole. A well-known Mexican cooking staple, mole is a complex and rich sauce made with a blend of dried chiles, spices, fruits and seasonings and used to add flavors to meats or dishes like enchiladas.

In creating the mole, Mi Tita would come to our house to assemble assembling the spices on a white plate. Sitting in the kitchen, I watched her do this. Mi Tita has some assistance from Doña Felipa or "Doña Fe," who was my nanny. So, Mi Tita gave Doña Fe directions and supervised her as she created the mole. At that time, I never thought about being a chef. I do remember being in the kitchen and watching Mi Tita cooking delicious meals for our family and Doña Fe.

One day, when I was about 13 or 14, I wanted to cook a dish. I asked Doña Fe if she could let me do the traditional dish known as sopa de fideo. A common meal to Mexican families, this is a soup made from tomatoes, angel hair pasta, garlic and vegetable broth. Doña Fe was hesitant to let me near anything to help. She told me that my Mom was going to kill her and I reassured her that wasn't going to happen. She acceded, and this was my first experience cooking in the kitchen. I never thought I was going to be a chef because I didn't have that feeling yet. That came with time. Imagine being a young girl, and all I wanted was to be in front of the stove and cook with my grandmother. As a kid, that's the last thing you want to do. It was more exciting to go outside and play with your friends.

ASSEMBLING INGREDIENTS FOR A CAREER

I discovered my culinary talent while in high school. My family asked me what I wanted to do in the future. On this topic, you get a lot of pressure. My dad actually picked my major in college. I had to get the nerve to tell him that his choice wasn't what I wanted to do.

I saw that the culinary field in Mexico was very popular and a top career choice. One day, my dad asked me what I finally wanted to do. Growing up in a Mexican family, my dad was super protective since I was his only daughter. I looked at many universities in other Mexican cities, and I thought that my dad wouldn't let me travel to attend one of those school but I determined to go. I told him that I wanted to be a chef, and he jokingly asked Doña Fe to teach me how to cook beans. I wasn't joking and said I'm visiting the Mexican Culinary Institute in Puebla.

We were impressed with the institute's large and attractive campus. The chefs dressed in super elegant white uniforms, and most of those attending were from Europe. None were Mexican. When the visit ended, I asked my dad what his decision was for me. He said, "It's what you decide." I liked it immediately, and I jumped for joy. That's when I had that special feeling that you get inside, that feeling that something is right. This is where I belong.

Here, the institute's program is for five years unlike what an American two-year college might offer. During those five years, students learn not only about preparing dishes, but also taking courses like marketing and administration that support this degree. Culinary arts is a career. I finished my coursework by traveling to Lyon, Paris, and graduated with a master's degree in pastry and in sommelier training. Being a sommelier refers to recommending wine varieties to diners, supervising wine serving and connecting with winemakers to review selections and prices. With a diploma, I returned by Mexico to plan my future with a little help.

I was always fascinated by tarot readings, so I met a reader who could tell me what was "in the cards" for me. She told me that my life was not to be in Mexico. I replied that my wish was to go to Europe to start my culinary career. She pointed that my destiny was to be in the United States. This was not the answer I wanted to hear. I was mad at her; I couldn't believe that I wasted my money on a reading. It was like putting money in the trash.

BUILDING A NEW LIFE AWAY FROM HOME

I thought about going back to Europe, especially Spain since it and Mexico have a shared language. My Dad had another idea: go to Chicago since I had family there. He wanted me to spend time with our cousins and then return to Mexico to open a restaurant. When I visited Chicago, I fell in love with the city. Chicago had more restaurants than houses and, therefore many culinary opportunities. So, I came with only $2,000 in my pocket, and I only knew a few English phrases. What helped me learn English was reading the Yellow Pages. It was there that I found a bilingual attorney who I contacted about what I needed to open a restaurant in Chicago. She charged me $5,000 and I would give her the $2,000. She found a space in Wicker Park. I went by the corner of Division and Damen and imagined myself owning a restaurant in that area. When I walked through that space, it was bar without a kitchen. I wanted to back out of this deal. It wasn't just because of the absence of a kitchen but because I didn't have the money.

The attorney was insistent, so I gave her the remaining balance and told her I would think about it. I immediately called my Dad and said to let's open his restaurant in Chicago. He thought I was joking; I wasn't. I thought it would be an easier process to open here. He asked if I didn't want to continue to live with the family in Mexico. In Mexican culture, the family always stays together. It doesn't matter if you 50 years old and unmarried or not, you live with your family. Imagine, I'm their only daughter, and I didn't want to continue living with them. My Dad asked if this was what I wanted; I said yes. He then asked if I had a business plan and how much money I needed to do this. This was the best day of my life. I was jumping for joy. I called back the attorney and said that I was interested in the property.

Imagine, I was going to be the executive chef and owner of my restaurant at a very young age—23. I didn't speak English and only had my experience from school. I hired people to run the waitstaff and I contacted a teacher from one of Chicago's best interior design schools to help me with the eatery's design. He created a contest to see which of his students could design it. I remember one student named Jeremy who won the contest, and he developed a very minimalistic design that conveyed a refined elegance defining Mexico and France. I chose Sabor Savour for the name. In Spanish, sabor means flavor, The French term of savour means to give flavor. Flavor, for me, is one of the most important things to have when presenting delicious meals. In my mind, the food could be from anywhere—Korea, India, America, or Mexico—but it has to taste good to one's palette. If the food doesn't taste good, no one will eat it.

We used gold, black and white for the color scheme, had gold candelabras on wood tables and an open kitchen situated in the middle of the restaurant. The latter was the place where both French and Mexican cuisines could come together. I wanted to avoid all art because the art comes to your table through the food. The food itself is very colorful. To me, the "first digestion" starts with your eyes. When someone puts a nice dish on your table, you're going to think it's delicious. Then you smell it, and you begin to salivate. When you finish eating, you complete the "second digestion," and this is where you take in the whole dining experience. As a chef, when those things happen, your mission is accomplished. Customers will have those pleasant and positive experiences that make them want to return for more.

My vision was to raise the bar of what many people consider Mexican cuisine. Here is America, when people think about Mexican food, they know Tex-Mex dishes like burritos and fajitas. When I came to this country, I didn't know about burritos, and when I saw them, it was too much. In culinary school, students learned French culinary techniques that could turn any dish preparation into a gourmet meal. It's like a whole other level. From what I'm seeing, we have a new generation of chefs from Mexico who are dedicated to share their talents and put our country on the map in this respect.

FROM COOKING TO CONSULTING

I only had Sabor Savour from 2009 to 2013. I can explain later what happened, but after I closed the restaurant, I received calls from others who wanted to hire me as a restaurant consultant. In this role, I talk with these business owners and learn what their visions are when they want to open their eateries. Some owners need to understand how to incorporate procedures and system or need more administrative assistance while others need with menu creation and a concept. I ask them questions such as who are their target customers, what is the price range for their food and where are the locations of their establishments. It all depends on what the owner wants.

I decided to go into the area because while I love being in a kitchen and in the restaurant industry, being a chef is not an easy job. You sacrifice your life. Working in a restaurant is a huge commitment; it's like caring for your family. You have to stay there every day 24/7. With consultation, there is no commitment. It's not a marriage. This way, I enjoy helping other people, and I have time to spend with my family.

Currently, I'm working with my mentor Mario on expanding his brand Bar Takito, an eatery offering Nuevo Latino American cuisine located near Chicago's West Fulton Market area. We want to work together as business partners and hope to open another location very soon. Mario, who has known me for 17 years, has been teaching me everything in relation to financials and other business topics and has seen me grow not only as a person but as a professional since I was 23.

RECEIVING WORLD RECOGNITION

Being recognized a Michelin-starred chef is like winning an Oscar for acting. This global European company is famously known for its tires and its chubby, friendly mascot of the Michelin Man. I received this distinction for Sabor Savour in 2011 and 2012. This award tells diners that the chef and the restaurant were evaluated and considered the best of the best.

I learned that I was chosen for this award when I working in the restaurant one evening. I talked with my host to see how the night went and then she gave me a manila envelope with the information. For some reason, I thought they wanted me to give them a gift certificate or money, and I wasn't about to give anything. I opened the envelope and found a formal letter. I asked someone to help me because it wasn't fluent in English. A staff member explained to me that Michelin recognized my eatery, mentioned a few of my dishes and me for its annual guide. With happiness brimming in my heart, I walked out crying and immediately called my family.

Michelin never alerts chefs or the restaurants as to when reviewers come. They are anonymous, so you have no idea. Nobody nominates you. The only way they know about you is through reviews.

I can't imagine how many chefs work so hard to get this achievement. Some of them are in the industry for years and never reach this. This recognition meant many things to me. It signifies passion, responsibility and love.

BLENDING THREE COMPONENTS INTO LEADERSHIP

Leadership is a tough word to define for me. Generally speaking, a leader is someone who is present and shows through example. Leadership is something that you are born with. Nobody teaches you this. It's part of your personality. If you have this ability, then people will follow you. You also have to seriously demonstrate the passion for what you are doing to others and the passion to deliver the message correctly for people to understand. If you don't properly deliver that message, people will not follow you. To be a good leader, you need to communicate well.

There also needs a sense of humility. If you think of yourself as a superstar or that you're the best, there are other people who believe they are better than you are. You can be very good at what you do, but you are developing your own style.

To be a leader, you need these three ingredients: humility, communications and a love of what you do. Without those, you're lost.

I live by one word: love. If you don't add love to what you do, you won't get the result you expect. Love is the key to everything. I discovered recently that I'm closer to God than from any other time, who is the essence of love. He is teaching me about love. I didn't have God in my past and my journey in building my career.

MAKING THE CHANGE FROM WITHIN

Believe in yourself. If you don't, then nobody else will. It all starts with you and even your thoughts. You choose what you want for your life. The problem is that we point fingers to others when things don't go right. That doesn't work. It's not the others, it's you. You have to change. I learned something from a conversation I had with my 16-year-old niece. I'm never going to forget it. We talked about life, and she said that it's about making choices. I said that's true. So, in my life, I choose to continue my goals, to be another person, and to believe in God. On this path, the choice is mine and no one else's.

I would encourage people to go for their goals, no matter what obstacles are in the road. If there are many, don't let those stop you. You will suffer and feel frustrated on that road because you're not reaching to goal immediately. Challenge yourself. To me, suffering is optional.

When it comes to experiencing failure, there are three times where this has occurred. The first was closing the doors to my highly successful, and Michelin recognized restaurant. That was due not having enough administrative experience, and there was a disagreement with the IRS. It accused me of not paying my taxes, but I did. In the end, I had to close.

The second time was in 2019 where I opened my second restaurant and we had five investors including myself. We had agreements in writing and lawyers handling the legal information. Unfortunately, people can trick you. I discovered I was locked out of the decision making process though I was the owner and operator. Then the COVID-19 pandemic came. As a result, the restaurant industry was shut down for two years. How was it going to come back? Luckily, I formed a small catering company where I delivered food during the weekends. The third failure came when a restaurant owner hired me to be a consultant to organize her business. She never paid me.

What I took away from all these situations is that failures make you stronger than before. It's your choice to stay down or you wake up and change your attitude to where you say "I don't care anymore. I'm going forward."

BIOGRAPHY

Yanitzin "Yanni" Sanchez will be the first to admit she eats and enjoys traditional Mexican foods — tortillas, frijoles, tacos but despite her Latin roots, she makes it abundantly clear that no one will ever find a humble burrito in her kitchen and instead will encounter the delicious and unique Mexican-French fusion flavors in her cuisine. Originally from Toluca, Mexico, she developed her culinary skills by experimenting with new tastes and trends she discovered while traveling throughout her home country and across Europe.

Despite her youth, Chef Yanni gained priceless experience while working at the Ritz Carlton in Paris and at the Mayan Palace in both Acapulco and Cancun, Mexico. She completed her training at the Ecole de Paris Patisserie Boulangère in Paris, France and owes her talents to her years of study at the Culinary Institute of Mexico in Puebla, where she graduated as Chef International. Chef Yanni currently resides in Chicago, IL where she works as a chef in the banquets area of the Art Institute of Chicago.

Yanitzin "Yanni" Sanchez

https://chefyanni.com

LinkedIn: Yanitzin Sanchez

THE BEGINNING OF YOUR LEADERSHIP JOURNEY

———

Ana Uribe-Ruiz

"The sky is never the limit; it is the beginning of a journey."

It has been said that "The sky is the limit." But you will see why my moto is a bit different. I was born and raised in Ecuador, where my dream of wings started. My dad was a visionary and formed an airline in the mid-1950s with a group of investors. The idea was to be part of that world, not as a pilot really because I never saw a woman in the cockpit, but in management. I have wanted to be an economist since I was little girl. My great aunt used to work at the Social Security Administration that my grandfather made possible when he was the mayor of the city, and remember her working on reports, making payments and so forth. Things changed along the way…

A LOSS OF A COMPANY

During the years of volatility in South American countries, Ecuador was one of those that had a couple of coup d'état. The military took control of the country and many things changed along the way. One of those was the airline that my father was part of. In 1974 under a decree, the air force took control of the company. It was closed in 2006.

TIME FOR A NEW LIFE

In my early twenties, my father's business went under. It was sad to see that happen, not only to him but to so many during the so called "war." We had a problem in the south of the country with Peru and things escalated. That made things very difficult for the companies and businesses that transacted in US dollars, especially for the airline industry. Small companies and places went under since the exchange rate went from 25 to 1 to 360 to 1 all in about a week.

I moved to the United States in my early twenties when things settled down a bit. My two brothers were in the United States, one graduated as an engineer, the second one was in the process. But boy, to keep up with mom and my brothers to make sure they had things for the last leg, as I called it, was tough. Lots of movement, things to be sold, finding a place to live, losing the house, the cars, and all was terrible. The legal side was another nightmare, but it got settled in some years. Dad stayed in the United States, but mom needed her family around and stayed in Ecuador, and my older brother moved back to establish his new family. That was the best for mom, a breather for me and my brother, who stayed behind.

A NEW BEGINNING

I love banks and love the way they work. I was a banker in Ecuador and then, when I moved to the United States, I wanted to study finance. Since my dream to be an economist went sideways, I ended up in law school. Who knew, right? I started working in the legal department at the local bank in Quito and I got so bored with so much paper, that I asked my boss if I could work opening accounts. It was a way to see people, to be part of the day-to-day activity, and not to be confined to a room with all this legal paperwork.

I moved to Florida, since it in was my backyard. That was the place that I spent every summer while my dad was working. I just enjoyed the city and the beaches. It was easy for me, since I knew where to go and what to look for. I returned to banking and learned a lot along the way, until I met my husband.

A NEW CHANGE

Our story is kind of different. I meet him during a phone call. Yes, a phone call. After that, we spoke every day for about six months. We never exchanged pictures, but our conversations always were open and honest. We had the same culture. We had the same language. We liked so many things and our visions were the same. We saw each other six months later and the rest is history, as they say. We planned a wedding, selected a date, and moved to New Jersey.

In that process, we realized the love of aviation was there for both of us. He was already a private pilot when I met him and we talked about someday doing the same, when time allows us to do so.

My son was born in 2001. But in mid-2003, we realized something was a bit different. Things were out of place. Something was telling me to get answers to all of my questions. We took him to be tested and he was diagnosed as autistic. The world change … again.

I put my energy into helping my son full time during his first couple of years to make sure his therapies were done, his language came along, his playtime was a bit different, the way he ate and what he found "tasty." There were struggles at the beginning, tantrums, looking for solutions and places to go, school, the education system and how it works. Really, what do I do? All in all, I always had a shoulder to lean on. My husband was amazing!

TIME TO FLY

We moved to California in 2009. The weather in California allows you to fly twelve months of the year. My husband got a new license and I started flying. The first flight was not pleasant because it was windy. But I had an amazing teacher, a certified flight instructor, who calmed me down and explained things in a way that made sense. I earned my license; and my husband and I decided it was time to get our own. Renting a plane for two people was too expensive, so financially, it was better to own a plane.

We love to fly together. One of the things we learned from the beginning, one of us is the pilot in command, the one who makes the decisions in the air. But we also understand that we can talk through something that we see and something that is different. If necessary, we adjust that flight plan. But the idea is always to get home to our son.

LET'S EMPOWER A NEW GENERATION

I am a firm believer that mentorship is key to make a change in an industry that has been difficult for women. Men traditionally have been the pilots, not women. We are a few who love to be in the air. But it is time to push the boundaries and bring more of us into this amazing world of aviation.

It all started when I was at flight school. I saw only men … in and out, the student, the instructors, the mechanics, all men. I decided to research why few women were pilots.

By an error on my part, I found Women of Aviation. It was such a surprise to see something out of the box to empower girls and women to fly and to be part of the aviation industry. I had a conversation with the founder. Mireille Goyer, a commercial airline pilot in Canada. Her mission has been from the beginning to give wings to the new generation. It is an organization without dues. You just learn to connect with aviators in your local area and give flights and talks during the month of March, because it represents the anniversary of the first license issued to a woman pilot.

It requires connections. And the great thing about aviation is, it is still a small world. People and places are all interconnected.

California has a lot of small airports. I am in the middle of Silicon Valley, which in my case, is the backdrop of the high-tech industry and its executives and wealthy families, who often have a way to fly. Small planes are all around us. And small airports are all over. The community of pilots is vast and large. With the conversation with Mireille, I needed to find a group of instructors or pilots with a commercial license, who had access to planes. After that, we chatted with the owners to see if they were willing to donate the flying time and to give girls and women a test of flight. The coordination took time and effort. It was the crazy me doing the things that I thought was necessary to show these girls about the dream of flight. My husband gave his time flying, too, because he was helping me along the way. What a crazy idea. But in 2013, we did it. Fifty girls and women flew with us. The challenge was how to make it more organized the next time around.

In 2014, I sat with a great friend, an air force veteran and author, who also likes to empower girls and see what we can do, to show those sitting in a corner in a class and not saying anything, those who want to be engineers and biologists, or because they want to be mechanics and pilots, or those who see something they want to be but do not have someone who looks like them to tell them the stories on how they got to do what they do. That, in itself, is **empowerment**.

That is the reason why we must think in a different way to show girls that if they want to learn science, let's introduce them to a scientist. If they want to be doctors, have a chat with one. That was the idea. So, that challenge grew larger, bolder, stronger. I got together with the flying club, the plane owners and a group of certified flight instructors, as well as pilots who wanted to give their time to show why we love to fly. Also, they wanted to show these young minds to think outside the box, outside their neighborhood, above the city they live and the place they are, that if they can see the world from above today, they also can make a change in their mind set and look for that dream they have. And the ones who do not really have an idea what to do next, allow them to explore new options.

The second challenge was to bring women who have been there before them, inspire the young with a flight and inspiration to be themselves in them. Because aviation is the center of this, it was necessary to bring people in that space: military pilots, commercial airline pilots, airport managers, controllers, and yes, the fun part, private pilots and acrobatic pilots.

The last challenge was to find all the girls. Thinking outside the box, a conversation with a teacher in the local middle school opens the door for a larger conversation. The principal who said yes to this crazy idea, the funding to get the girls by bus from and to school, and the blessing of the superintendent came next.

Everything lined up to do this. When all of the girls came, that was the problem ... all of the reservations totaled 350. WOW! Now, how do we put all this together? The idea was three days. So, back to the drawing board, which made it a full week. Remember that I needed to have the pilots who had the time. That also was a challenge because many of them work full time. So, the coordination was crazy. I had three weeks to do this.

It was advertised locally, and the news media came, including local stations. The Veterans Administration also came and gave us a platform to do the question-and-answer session of this amazing women life online, so things came together, and then on the 3rd day, the club that I was working with, had an issued with a CFI and stop the use of the planes until they found a solution. What do we do? Why now? What happened?

That is when the connections came into play. A mass email was sent to the plane owners and pilots in two different airports, telling them what happened and that I have these girls in the wind. "We must make it to the end to find a solution" was my goal. They responded with extra planes and pilots, all in about three hours. On Sunday, the last day of flights, young pilots rented planes and made the last flights. Aviation is a large family. When things are needed, people step up.

The icing on the cake, as they say, came later. I received small notes from each girl, who told me how much this meant to them. They expressed their visions of getting into math classes and learning more to be engineers later in life, of having a voice in choosing the classes for tomorrow, or management was in their mind, and college was the first step. That is what it is all about. Empower them to make their choices for their future. I realized that they have it and they can make a change. They needed that focus to get to where they wanted to go and a person who was available to empower them to do it. That is not easy, and the push back is big. But they are bigger than that, that they got this!

My surprise? I was nominated for the Jefferson Award for Public Service. The reason? The empowerment to bring women into the aviation industry. It was here that I realized it is not only the flights, it was the conversations with these girls to give them a view of what they can be tomorrow. That we need more of them, which is not going to be easy. College will be first, flying after. It takes money and time to go into this industry and that requires dedication, finances and a mindset that they can do this, and they belong here.

Remember that saying that the sky is the limit? Well, it is not. That is why my moto is:

"The sky is never the limit; it is the beginning of a journey."

BIOGRAPHY

Ana Uribe-Ruiz, co-president of Women in Aviation's San Francisco Bay Area Chapter, was born and raised in Quito, Ecuador. Aviation was always part of her life. In the 1950s, her father formed an airline, called Ecuatoriana de Aviación, in late 1950s that was the flag airline for the country for many years.

For her and her brothers, flying from one place to another was the norm. She spent time with her dad and his captains in the cockpit and she was able to see their world with a different view. She went to law school and then she moved to the United States in the early 1980s to study finance and become a banker. Banking and Insurance has been part of her life for many years. When she got married, her husband had a private pilot license, so the idea to flying together came about. That changed when their son was diagnosed as autism. She then became involved with the special needs community in New Jersey and did the same when they moved to California. The weather here was key to start her pilot training and was a way to enjoy her time with her husband flying around the state, especially since their son was settled at school and doing amazing.

She became incredibly involved with Women of Aviation International Week and became the only private pilot who has a Jefferson Award for Public Service for bringing women into the aviation world in the Bay Area. She is immensely proud of that accomplishment, which she received in March 2014.

The aviation industry needs to have more of women out there and she is often talking and presenting in schools about aviation, its relationship to STEM, and inspiring the future generation of pilots. Mentorship is key, so the next generation will take us further into the aviation and aerospace industry.

Ana Uribe-Ruiz
LinkedIn: anauriberuiz
IG: @acuriberuiz

SERVANT LEADERSHIP: THE WAY TO IMPACT

Jacqueline S. Ruiz

"The most beautiful gift you can give others is the gift of service."

My *familia* is very small. I am the only girl of three siblings and the youngest. My two older brothers are seven and eleven years older than I am, so I always felt as if I was an only child.

My mother dreamed of having a girl and thought I would be less energetic than her two crazy boys, but it turned out to be completely the opposite! She quickly realized that I had more energy than the two boys combined!

Growing up with an alcoholic father was difficult due to financial struggles, lack of support, and violence at my house. My brothers grew up and decided to leave for the United States to find a better life while my mother and I stayed with my dad in a very small town in the center of Mexico. While my brothers were trying to find their purpose and a better life for us in another country, my dad would disappear for days which would make us think the worst. Those were dark times of violence and despair, but I somehow would find my escape in books. The self-development books would offer me a totally new perspective on life, especially of the life that I was experiencing at that moment.

I felt something inside of me that wanted to make a difference in the world, but my reality was not favorable at all. All I could do is dream and get lost in the literature that I would read every day. That is when I first learned about leadership. With books as my guide, I would take initiative to host toy drives in my neighborhood, oftentimes donating the little money that I had. I would invite kids to my house to teach them what I was learning from those amazing books and host contests to share that information. Even in my small way, I started feeling more connection with acts of service in the community. It felt good to help and share my knowledge.

Eventually, my dad's alcoholism became unbearable. My mom decided to take matters into her own hands and leave that small town to be reunited with my two brothers in the United States. I still remember the day that my mom told my father. It was a decision that had been made. There was no way to change her mind at that point.

My dad came to me and asked me, with alcohol in his

breath, "Do you really want to go to the United States?" I replied with the conviction of a fourteen-year-old girl determined to achieve her dreams, "Yes, Dad, that is the one thing that I want more than anything in the world. I have so much that I want to do in life. I want to change the world and I cannot do it in this small town. I want to achieve the American dream."

He looked at me and realized that I was truly determined. He knew that if he did not take effective steps to become sober and join us, he would lose us forever. That day, that conversation, marked the end of my dad's drinking. It has been twenty-five years and my dad is still sober today. The conviction of a small girl with big dreams can change the world—at least someone's world. About ten years later, my dad and I had another conversation about that day and how it changed his life forever. He remembered the spark in my eyes when I was talking about my dreams in the land of opportunity and how inspired he was. He thanked me for saving his life.

THAT FEELING HAD A NAME: SERVANT LEADERSHIP

Years laters, that determination and desire to succeed along with hardwork and action, I became an entrepreneur. At age twenty-three, I opened up my own marketing firm. My love for helping others reach their dreams and my love for creativity in marketing was a perfect combination and segway into creating something of my own. I continued to develop my mind and business through personal and professional development any chance I could.

The first time I heard the concept of "servant leadership" my heart beeped with excitement. It was like listening to the most beautiful melody. I was at an event where a hospital CEO introduced this concept and I fell in love. I started researching it more and the more I knew, the more intrigued I was. Could I be a servant leader? Could I make my leadership style through service? That sounded perfectly aligned with my mission, both personally and in business. The person who coined this term said it was the idea of being a leader through acts of service and inspiration. It was amazing to be able to recognize this style of leadership in words, as throughout my life I was always leading with kindness and acts of service. It was a day I will never forget.

EVERYTHING IS CONNECTED

As life continued on, that curious and energetic girl was always inside me. I loved trying new things and in 2015 I fell in love with the world of aviation. I was attending a hot air balloon show, when I spotted a small airplane in the sky. Afterwards, I bought a discovery flight, and was immediately captivated. It would be a few more months until the "divine download" or inspiration to get my pilot's license would come to me. But when it came, my life changed...

I had no idea of how fascinating and challenging getting my pilot's license would be, but most importantly, how many people I would be able to inspire through this achievement. I remember the day of my first solo flight and the teddy bear a friend of mine had given me as a symbol of companionship and bravery. That was a beautiful act of kindness that I wanted to replicate and spread to others. Since then, I have given away over 1,500 teddy bears to young people, nonprofit organizations, and grown adults around the world to encourage them and for them to know they are not alone.

As I continued flying I never missed an opportunity to spread inspiration, take people flying, or share the magic of aviation with them. I became a certified "young eagles" pilot, which allowed me to be able to take young kids up in the air for the first time. This was a wonderful way to service the community and I loved every minute of it!

LIVE TO SERVE AND SERVE TO LIVE

My world of aviation was not slowing down and I was so excited to continue flying. On one special occasion, I invited two other fellow Latina pilots to join me at a celebration to give airplane rides and inspiration to the local communities near the airports I used for my flights. The airport of the event was only about an eighteen-minute flight from my home airport. I arrived at 6:00 a.m. to prepare the plane, fuel it up, and take off. The weather was calm and beautiful.

I arrived at the destination airport without any issues after a short eighteen-minute flight. We debriefed the route of the flights with our fellow pilots. Our guests arrived along with local dignitaries and media. The event was a success! Three Latina pilots flying passengers—a rare sight.

Afterwards, I flew back to my home airport. I knew that a storm was coming from that direction, but it would not hit for a few hours later. I kissed my husband goodbye on the runway before taking off as he drove back home. As soon as I took off, I felt the weather change. I had to decide either to come back to that airport now with a strong crosswind or proceed to my home airport. I decided on the latter. Little did I know that I was about to experience the worst day of my life as a pilot.

For the remainder of the flight I felt fear, but I kept flying the airplane. I will confess that there was a time during the flight where I was ready to succumb to mother nature and let go of the airplane controls as I could not bear the fear any longer. For a split second, I thought about what would be my grave—the river or the football field below. My entire life flashed before my eyes, and I could not help but think about my kids back at home. That could not be the last time I ever saw them!

Runway two seven seemed so close, but at the same time so far away. I made the decision that I was going to face my fear and land smooth as butter. I kept flying the plane, shaking, but never letting go of the controls. A good pilot never lets go of the controls. I needed to stay strong. I communicated with the tower to submit a PIREP (pilot's report on weather), so that they could alert other nearby planes. I wanted to land and touch the ground as soon as possible.

Despite my fear, I made the decision to land on runway two seven. I knew that the turbulence would intensify closer to the ground, but I was determined. Time seemed to slow down as I kept flying the plane, staying focused on my mission. I continued to feel every bump, every air bubble, and the plane shook from the wind. I did not let go of the controls for one minute. I was laser focused and ready to kiss the solid ground as soon as I landed. Thankfully, I had accumulated over one hundred hours of flight and several hundred landings in my training with several private instructors. That preparation ultimately led me to land safely.

I came home shaken with the realization that my life could have been over. I rang the doorbell of the main door so that my husband would come to greet me and embrace me in his arms, since I was so startled and moved by the experience. The rest of the day was spent in bed, sometimes crying, and thinking how blessed I was to be alive.

After some time of rest, I decided to direct my energy to another activity. I could not stay in bed for the rest of my life! That is not my nature, and it is not the first time that I experience something bad that moves me to the core. I did what I know best—intensify my gratitude in difficult times. I went to the grocery store to buy ingredients to prepare meals for the rest of the week. I turned my fear and adversity into a creative energy for cooking delicious meals. Most importantly, I also made the decision to not give up on my hobby of aviation and to reach for my next milestone.

For the next few weeks, I spent a lot of time at the airport—both day and night—flying bigger, faster, and more stable planes. Currently, I am almost done with all the prerequisites for my second pilot's license! This means I can fly different and more advanced aircrafts.

TODAY'S INSPIRED LEADER VOLUME IV

When you experience turbulence (both in the air and in life) and you cannot control it, you must arm yourself with strength, vision, and grit. You must think of the landing as your destination, you must think of your why; you must create a purpose that is bigger than you to get you over the fear of the situation.

Maybe you are not in a life-or-death situation. Perhaps you are just taking off on your dreams. You are landing a little rough on your goals or you are afraid of making decisions. Although you do not know what to do at any given moment, you are equipped with purpose, strength, and vision. This is what gets you to your destination. This is what allows you to truly show up as a leader. When it comes to leadership, especially servant leadership, it is about showing up for yourself and others in the critical moments.

TRANSCEND NOW AND ALWAYS

I am 100% certain that every human can make sound decisions that create legacy and transcendence. I am 100% certain that every individual regardless of age, background, or upbringing can answer the call of leadership. I instill in my children the power of taking action that elevates others—to serve others, to pick up the garbage when they see it on the ground, to lend a hand when someone is in need, to open the door for others, to give a smile, to spread acts of kindness.

Ever since I had another chance to live at the age of twenty three after hearing the word "cancer" in my body twice and going through a multitude of surgeries, procedures, tests, doctors' visits… something shifted in me. A sense of urgency to live to serve others was born. I recognized that my life was a gift and I had to be a gift to others. I committed to God and promised to renew my gratitude contract with him every single day through my acts of kindness. That's how I pay it forward. There is not a day that goes by that I do not think of how lucky and blessed I am to be alive. I do not take it for granted. I am honored to live the life I have and I will continue to serve, lead, and inspire. I invite you to think about these questions to further understand how you can live with purpose, transcend and truly create impact.

- What can you do today to renew your own gratitude contract?
- How many people can you touch this week through acts of kindness?
- How are you being called to or desire to live your life of leadership?

The answer is in your heart.

CLOSE YOUR EYES AND DO

It's important to mention that there are many ways to "live" your leadership, but it must begin with authenticity. It is said that when the alignment of words and action is present, all is possible. If you had a group of people in front of you and you were asked which of those individuals was more grateful or valued family the most, you would not be able to tell by simply how they look.

TODAY'S INSPIRED LEADER VOLUME IV

You would have to observe them for a period of time to see how their actions align with those values. You would have to identify patterns, behaviors, and even habits to then select the individual that represents those particular attributes. By the same token, a servant leader must be aligned with their values through their actions; that is where congruency is present. That is when trust is built. That is when reliability is generated.

What is the most important thing to you? What moves you? What are the core values that must absolutely be present? What are your non-negotiables?

Start by making a list of your core values or non-negotiables down. Then, write down the actions of how they will come to life in your daily actions. Put reminders on your calendar. Start taking those small actions and steps. Monitor your progress. Take time to reflect how you are living your core values every day. After 30 days, evaluate and grade yourself. If you identify gaps, fill them. Work harder the next 30 days. If all checks out, then you are living your authentic truth as a leader.

BIOGRAPHY

Jacqueline Ruiz is a visionary social entrepreneur that has created an enterprise of inspiration. With more than 20 years of experience in the marketing and public relations industry, she has created two successful award-winning companies, established two nonprofit organizations, published 31 books—the largest collection of Latina stories in a book anthology series in the world—and held events in four continents. She has received over 30 awards for her contributions and business acumen.

Jacqueline is currently the CEO of award-winning JJR Marketing, one of the fastest-growing top marketing and public relations agencies in Chicago, and Fig Factor Media, an international media publishing company that helps individuals bring their books to life. Jacqueline is also the Founder of The Fig Factor Foundation, a not-for-profit organization dedicated to giving vision, direction, and structure to young Latinas (ages 12-25), as well as the President of Instituto Desarrollo Amazing Aguascalientes, the first youth center in Calvillo, Aguascalientes,

Mexico, offering various hands-on experience, courses, and global connections to support the local troubled youth in defining their dreams.

Jacqueline currently serves as a board member for the The Fig Factor Foundation, the Alumni Executive Board at the College of DuPage, LovePurse and the World Leaders Forum. She is a recent graduate of the DePaul University Women Entrepreneurship Cohort 3 and the Stanford University Graduate School of Business, Latino Business Action Network Cohort 11. She represents 1.6% of women entrepreneurs with over seven figures in the United States.

Jacqueline is one of the very few Latina sports airplane pilots in the United States and the founder of Latinas in Aviation global brand. She believes that "taking off is optional, landing on your dreams is mandatory."

Jacqueline S. Ruiz
www.jackiecamacho.com
IG: pilotina_offical

Made in the USA
Middletown, DE
16 February 2023

24249138R00109